HEALING OF
MEMORIES

/////

HEALING *of*

MEMORIES

DAVID A. SEAMANDS

VICTOR BOOKS®

A DIVISION OF SCRIPTURE PRESS PUBLICATIONS INC.
USA CANADA ENGLAND

Fifth printing, 1989

Unless otherwise noted, Scripture quotations are from the *New American Standard Bible,* © The Lockman Foundation 1960, 1962, 1963, 1971, 1972, 1973, 1975, 1977. Other quotations are from the *Holy Bible, New International Version* (NIV), © 1973, 1978, 1984 by the International Bible Society. Used by permission of Zondervan Bible Publishers; the *King James Version* (KJV); *The New Testament in Modern English* (PH), © by J.B. Phillips, permission of Macmillan Publishing Co. and Collins Publishers; *The Holy Bible: Revised Standard Version* (RSV), © 1952 by the Division of Christian Education of the National Council of the Churches of Christ in the United States.

Recommended Dewey Decimal Classification: 200.19 or 152.42
Suggested Subject Heading: PASTORAL PSYCHOLOGY

Library of Congress Catalog Card Number 85-50310
ISBN: 0-89693-169-2

VICTOR BOOKS
A division of SP Publications, Inc.
Wheaton, Illinois 60187

CHAPTER ONE · 9
The Mystery of Memory

CHAPTER TWO · 23
What Is Healing of Memories?

CHAPTER THREE · 33
Why Do Some Memories Need Healing?

CHAPTER FOUR · 43
Creating the Atmosphere for Healing

CHAPTER FIVE · 61
Biblical Foundations for Memory Healing

CHAPTER SIX · 79
Indications for the Healing of Memories

CHAPTER SEVEN · 95
Distorted Concepts of God

CHAPTER EIGHT · 107
Difficulties from the Distortions about God

CHAPTER NINE · 123
Preparing for the Prayer Time

CHAPTER TEN · 139
Conducting the Prayer Time

CHAPTER ELEVEN · 163
Healing Memories of Sexual Traumas

CHAPTER TWELVE · 181
Follow-up, Cautions, and Conclusions

CONTENTS

To my many counselees
who honored me with their trust,
enriched me by their sharing,
and taught me most of what I know
about the miracle of inner healing.

MEMORIES are not simply mental pictures of the past. Rather, they are present experiences of the total person . . . feelings, concepts, attitudes, and behavior patterns. Thus they tend to make us repeat those actions which accompany the pictures on the screen of our minds.

This is the way the Bible speaks of memory when it urges God's people to call something to remembrance. Scripture never compartmentalizes us into physical, mental, and spiritual beings, but emphasizes the life of the whole person.

The real tragedy of hurtful memories is not simply the emotional pain they bring or the powerful push from the past we feel within us. Rather, it is because of the pain and the push, we learn wrong ways of relating to people and coping with life. In time, these become our very personality patterns —our way of life.

Time alone cannot heal the memories of experiences so painful they have been pushed out of our conscious minds. They require a special kind of spiritual therapy. This includes a period of counseling and preparation, a session of deep healing prayer, and a time of follow-up for relearning.

Healing of Memories is for lay people who want to be free of painful memories which affect present behavior and Christian growth. It is also for professionals who want to help others be free of the tyranny of the past.

DAVID A. SEAMANDS
WILMORE, KENTUCKY

PREFACE

1
THE MYSTERY OF MEMORY

Mɪᴛᴢɪ ᴡᴀѕ ᴇxᴄɪᴛᴇᴅ. "It's all beginning to make sense —the pieces are fitting together. At least now I understand *where* I need help and *what* I need to be praying about. And there's hope—no, better than that—Harry and I *know* there's healing ahead and that's making such a big difference in everything."

I couldn't keep from liking this fine young couple— both so attractive and intelligent, obviously deeply in love with one another, and strongly committed to the highest ideals of a Christian marriage. But like so many others, they had discovered from the very start that they couldn't seem to keep from hurting and being hurt by each other. As we counseled together, it became clear that the heart of the problem was Mitzi's hypersensitivity and her unrealistic expectations. Some people have been described as "accidents waiting to happen." It seemed

that Mitzi was one deep reservoir of pain waiting to be
tapped into. All her life, pastors and teachers had told
her to just forget the past, claim victory in Christ, and
develop new skills for coping with the present and future.

So Mitzi was surprised when I encouraged her not only
to become aware of the painful memories but even to
write them down so she could share them with me and
her husband. She did this conscientiously and prayerfully.

Now we both felt the time was ripe and so had sched-
uled the in-depth healing prayer session. One by one,
Mitzi visualized before the Lord some of her most hurtful
and humiliating childhood and teenage experiences. As
we prayed, our imaginations were literally "back there" in
time. She was not simply remembering the past. She was
reliving and refeeling incidents, often in remarkable detail, *as if she were actually there now.* Although it was a
struggle, Mitzi was forgiving the many people who had
hurt her; and in turn, she was receiving God's forgiveness
for her long-held resentments against them.

When, during the prayer time there was a long unex-
pected pause, I gently suggested that if the Spirit was
showing her something new, she should go ahead and
share it with the Lord. The tone of her voice became that
of a little child as she began her prayer, "Dear Jesus," and
told Him something she had not remembered for many
years. She was about four years old and, together with her
family, was visiting her grandmother. Grandma had wov-
en a tiny blanket for her doll. Mitzi was a painfully shy
child. It was almost impossible for her to even say "hello"
"hi" or "thank you" to anyone. When Grandma gave her
the blanket, her parents said, "Isn't that nice of Grandma
to work so hard and make such a pretty blanket for your
dolly? Now Mitzi, tell her thank you." Mitzi whimpered
out her childish prayer, "O Jesus, You know how badly I

wanted to say thanks to Grandma, but there was a big lump in my throat and I just couldn't say it. Dear Jesus, I tried so hard, but it wouldn't come out."

Now Mitzi shook with sobs. I tried to comfort her, asked her to imagine herself sitting on Jesus' lap, like the children in the Bible. This gave her the necessary encouragement to go on. The deepest hurt was yet to come. "My little sister was there and said she wanted the blanket. So Mother and Dad told me if I didn't say thank you, they'd give it to her. And when I couldn't say it, they did. They gave it to Patti! *O Jesus, You know how much I wanted to say it. But no one understood, no one cared. It's not fair, it's not fair!"*

As we continued praying, Mitzi saw how much this and other similar experiences had influenced her life. She had allowed deep bitterness to enter her heart. She had carried it against her parents and her sister. Now it had become the pattern of her life. Whenever she sensed injustice or misunderstanding, she became tongue-tied, filled with bitterness, and unable to communicate. Thus she could never resolve problems. In subsequent sessions, we worked together to help her learn new ways of openness with Harry and with other people. To this day, Mitzi insists that that time of healing prayer was the turning point of her life.

What happened to Mitzi and the many others we shall be describing? They had a deep experience of Christ which brought about the healing of festering memories which had been poisoning their inner lives and their outer relationships with others. This experience is what many of us call the healing of memories and what this book is all about. But before we go further, I want us to take a general look at the subject of memory itself, as seen by modern science and in the Scriptures.

Memory in Scripture

The Bible deals with the awesome power of memory in the same way it does many other concepts—with very little description or theoretical discussion. In a complete concordance of the Scriptures, you will find the noun *memory* listed less than half a dozen times. When a memory becomes something more concrete, like a *memorial*, it jumps up to twenty-five references. But when it becomes a verb as *to remember*, or *call to mind a remembrance*, then there are over 250 such references. About seventy-five of them refer to God and His memory. Many of them are requests for God to remember something—His covenants, His promises, or His people. Or they are requests for Him *not* to remember something—sins, failures, and the like. The remaining 175 describe the memory or the forgetfulness of people. Among these are many commands to remember or not to remember certain important matters.

In Scripture, memory is considered one of the most important aspects of both God's mind and ours. It is central to God's nature as well as to forgiveness, salvation, and righteous living. God's ability to remember or not remember is a part of the divine mind or knowledge which filled the biblical writers with awe. Since we have been created in the divine image, we too have this ability. Though ours is limited, the biblical writers considered this human facility a reason for wonder and praise.

Take, for example, Psalm 139. While the awestruck psalmist begins by contemplating the vastness of God's mind and His ability to know and remember everything, he soon switches over to himself. He is amazed at how the Creator has made him. "Such knowledge is too wonderful for me, too lofty for me to attain. . . . I praise You because I am fearfully and wonderfully made; Your works are wonderful, I know that full well" (Psalm 139:6, 14, NIV).

How amazingly accurate God's Word is. For to this very day, the most brilliant scientists, doctors, and psychologists are hard-pressed even to formulate theories on memory. This, in spite of the fact that it is the basis of almost everything we do in life.

The Incredible Giant

What is this mysterious process we call memory? How are we able to recall mental pictures of places and people we experienced years ago? Our immediate answer is that the past is all stored somewhere in the brain. But what we've done is to answer one mystery with another! For in spite of great advances in research during the last fifty years, the brain remains the most unexplainable part of our human equipment. When the *Reader's Digest* published its famous series on the various parts and functions of the body, it began with the brain. It classified it, along with the heart and lungs, as *one* of the giants of the body. We now know it is *the* giant; for while you can be kept alive by an artificial heart and lungs, there is no substitute for the brain. The legal definition of death is when brain activity ceases. There are times when the brain's activities slow down and relax, but they never stop as long as we're alive.

The brain itself is about three pounds of "messy substance shut in a dark warm place—a pinkish-gray mass, moist and rubbery to the touch, about the size of a soft ball" (*Our Human Body*, the Reader's Digest Association, p. 99). Perched like a flower on top of a slender stalk— the spinal cord—it is connected by the finest fibers to every nook and cranny of our bodies, from the roots of our hair and teeth to the tips of our fingers and toes. It is the center of the most elaborate communication network in all of creation. Statistics from medical scientists boggle the mind. There are an estimated 13 billion nerve cells inside the brain itself. Most of those cells make contact with, that is, have junctions with 5,000 other nearby nerve cells. Some have as many as 50,000 such junctions or *synapses*. The word *astronomical* isn't big enough to describe this, for the number of connections inside one brain far exceeds the number of stars in all the galaxies! But that's only the beginning.

The informers of the brain are our sense organs, posted like sentinels at strategic points throughout the body. Take the skin, for example. In it are 4 million structures sensitive to pain, 500,000 which detect touch or pressure and another 200,000 which keep track of the temperature. Add the *big ones* to this—the ears, eyes, nose, and tongue—and you are beginning to get the picture. The best way to picture the brain's network is to imagine thousands of telephone switchboards, each one big enough for a city like New York or London. Every circuit is operating at full capacity, receiving requests and plugging them into the proper circuit in a fraction of a second. This is only a faint idea of what takes place in your brain when you do the simplest daily tasks, like remembering a friend's address.

A Little Lower Than God

You can see why memory is called a mystery. For though memory is rooted in this incredible brain system, it is also a part of the mind which is above and beyond the network. The human mind is greater than and distinct from the system through which it operates.

Scientists who enter brain research soon find themselves involved in philosophical theory which goes far beyond the purely material. Deep questions surface: How does the brain, a physical substance, interrelate and interact with the mind, a nonmaterial reality? How do our emotional attitudes and our spirits affect our bodies and minds the way they do?

The Bible is not a scientific textbook and does not give us formal answers to such questions. Instead, it gives us a picture of the whole person as created by God. Although we are made in God's image, we can no more fully understand all about our own minds than we can possibly understand God's mind. When the Scripture talks about body, soul, and spirit, it takes for granted the full *unity* of a human being. Nowhere does it isolate a person's brain from the rest of the personality, anymore than it isolates the body or the soul. It always emphasizes the whole life of a person.

Have we gotten away from the subject of memories? No, for memories are the experiences of whole persons as they remember something, and not simply brain-stored pictures of the past. Memories include feelings, concepts, patterns, attitudes, and tendencies toward actions which accompany the pictures on the screen of the mind. This is the way the Bible uses the concept of remembrance, or stirring us up to remember something. When Scripture commands us to "remember the Lord," it does not mean to simply have a mental picture of God. It is a command to whole persons to orient all our thoughts and actions around God. The same is true when it tells us to "remember our Creator in the days of our youth." Or "remember the Sabbath Day to keep it holy." This is far from simply asking us to engage in mental or spiritual exercises in thinking and reflecting. It's an appeal to whole persons to set certain priorities and to live according to spiritual principles of worship and action.

This wholistic idea of memory is in complete accordance with all the latest findings in brain and behavior research. The tendency now is to look on the entire body as an extension of the brain, almost as if each cell of the body were a miniature brain/mind in itself. Everything is connected and interrelated. As with the circulation of the blood, so information and instructions, giving and receiving of responses, flow back and forth from the brain to all parts of the body. Related to all of this and *yet transcending it*, is the unique selfhood of individual persons.

In the *King James Version* of Psalm 8:5, we read that God has made man "a little lower than the angels." But the newer translations render it more accurately with, "Thou hast made him a little lower than God." Truly it is this remarkable gift of memory which enables us to gather all the knowledge of the past and use it in our imaginations to create new and wonderful pictures for the future. No wonder the psalmist goes on to exult in his status:

Thou . . . dost crown him with glory
    and majesty. . . .
Thou hast put all things under his feet. . . .
O Lord, our Lord,
How majestic is Thy name in all the earth!
                                    (Psalm 8:5, 6, 9)

Where Do Memories Begin?
Verse 2 of Psalm 8 contains those famous words, "From the mouth of infants and nursing babes Thou has established strength." Only in the last few years have we come to realize the truth of those words in reference to memo-

ry. Again and again I have been amazed at the power which painful memories from infancy seem to have in adult experience. Years ago when I first began the ministry of inner healing, I was very skeptical of these early memories. Slowly but surely, I have been forced to abandon my skepticism and in several instances have had to pray for the healing of some memories which could only have begun before birth. One young man was not healed of his almost compulsive recurrences of suicidal depression until his mother finally told him she had witnessed the suicide of a family member, when she was almost eight months pregnant with him. He had kept talking about strange and terrifying scenes of death which we could never trace. Now we prayed for the Holy Spirit to heal whatever evil influences that experience had on him. We asked God to heal all the roots of the family tree, changing it from a tree of death to a tree of life. It was the beginning of his release from fear and depression.

People who have been adopted need to make peace with that fact. It doesn't matter if they've had the finest set of parents in the world. I said almost these very words one day to Mavis as she sat in my office. God had been doing miracles of healing in her life, but there were still some areas which disturbed her. Mavis loved her stepfather deeply and had a good relationship with him. She had never known her real father, who had died before she was born. Mavis was a brilliant student with a keen and logical mind, and what I was saying sounded quite "off the wall" to her. But she agreed to read chapter 12 from my book, *Healing for Damaged Emotions*, which tells the story of Betty. This is how Mavis described the painful yet healing experience which took place.

Suddenly and without warning, tears began to flow down my cheeks as I sat reading the story of Betty. Her dad had left her when she was three and a half years old. During a healing session with Dr. Seamands, she had uttered this painful cry to her daddy (as if she were a child again), "O Daddy, please don't leave me!"

I identified with these words so personally as I read them. They came alive and touched something deep within me, something I had not realized was there. It was as if I were the one who had uttered them over twenty-two years ago, while still in my mother's womb. You see, my father died of cancer three months before I was born.

Not understanding all that was happening to me, I decided to go and take a walk. These strange tears and emotions were too strong, too real to be ignored or repressed. For the next hour I slowly wandered about town during the early evening hours. I resolved to let myself feel whatever might arise from within me. And feelings concerning my father's death came in abundance. To say the least, they surprised me.

It was as if I were actually back within my mother's womb at the hospital bedside of my father. Inside the womb I fought to be heard, to somehow be acknowledged. I kicked and struggled with all my might so my father could see me, touch me, hold me, kiss me, love me before he died. Over and over again I kept saying, "Daddy, please don't die, please don't die. *Please* don't die. You haven't even seen me yet. You don't even know if I'm a boy or a girl. O Daddy, please don't die!"

As I continued to walk, the tears never

seemed to subside. For the first time in my life,
I was mourning the death of my father. A few
tears had fallen at the thought of his death, as I
had grown up, but never had I experienced such
emotion and meaning in my ·tears and pain.
Now, as an adult, I was. experiencing the same
anguish and struggle as I did many years ago,
while I was in my mother's womb.

Even still, I am skeptical as I think of a
prebirth infant mourning the death of her father. Yet I cannot deny the thoughts, emotions,
and healing I experienced so unexpectedly.
They were simply too deep, too real, too spon-
taneous to be denied.

Time magazine of August 15, 1983 carried a cover story
on "Babies, What Do They Know? When Do They Know
It?" Reporting on hundreds of medical and behavioral
experiments being conducted in the United States,
France, Austria, as well as in other parts of the world, the
article described

an enormous campaign aimed at solving one of
the most fascinating riddles of human life: What
do newborn children know when they emerge
into this world? And how do they begin organiz-
ing and using that knowledge during the first
years of life? . . . The basic answer, which is
repeatedly being demonstrated in myriad new
ways: *Babies know a lot more than most people
used to think. They see more, hear more, understand more, and are genetically prewired to make
friends with any adult who cares for them* (pp. 52-
53, italics mine).

One of the most important results of these studies is the conclusive proof that long before an infant can speak, he is thinking and learning and remembering. As this article states, "Intellect is at work long before any language is available as a tool. . . . Babies develop an important ability to recognize categories. This was once thought to require language—how can the unnameable be identified? But babies apparently can organize perceptions without a word." The article goes on to show how children very early learn their own unspoken language of shapes, sounds, colors, smells, as well as a language of responses and relationships with people. They *remember an amazing variety of specific things long before they can speak or have words to identify objects or people.*

How far back can we push the frontiers of memory? The *Time* article states, "The search for data is being steadily pushed back from childhood to earliest infancy *and even before birth!"* (p. 53, italics mine)

Dr. Thomas Verny, a Canadian neurologist and psychiatrist, makes a strong case for prebirth memory in his best-selling book, *The Secret Life of the Unborn Child.* Dr. Verny traces the prenatal development of the child and comes to this conclusion:

> The first thin slivers of memory track begin streaking across the fetal brain sometime in the third trimester, though exactly when is hard to pinpoint. Some investigators claim a child can remember from the sixth month on; others argue the brain does not acquire powers of recall until the eighth month. There is, however, no question that the unborn child remembers or that he retains his memories. . . . We can safely deduce that certainly from the sixth month after

conception his central nervous system is capable of receiving, processing, and encoding messages. Neurological memory is most assuredly present at the beginning of the last trimester, when most babies, if born, can survive with the help of incubators (Summit Books, pp. 142, 191).

Dr. Verny documents his claims with scores of interesting illustrations of both prenatal and very early infant memories.

To many of us this sounds farfetched, but it didn't to our grandparents who accepted prenatal influence as a matter of fact, though they carried it to ridiculous extremes. I can still hear my grandmother suggesting to a neighbor that perhaps the reason why a certain little boy down the street had such a long, ugly nose was that his mother had visited the zoo too often and spent too much time watching the elephants! But we are discovering that a lot of those old wives' tales contained a kernel of truth. Most primitive peoples are careful to keep expectant mothers away from frightening experiences.

In a carefully controlled study of 2,000 women during pregnancy and birth, Dr. Monika Lukesch, of Constantine University in Frankfurt, West Germany, came to the conclusion that *the mother's attitude toward her baby has the greatest single effect on how an infant turns out.* And just as important, Dr. Lukesch found that the quality of a woman's relationship with her husband rates second and has a decisive effect on the unborn child.

Dr. Gerhard Rottmann, of the University of Salzburg in Austria, came to much the same conclusion; he even showed that the unborn child is capable of very fine emotional distinctions. This is illustrated by the biblical story in which the Virgin Mary visits her cousin Elizabeth to tell her of the visit of the angel and the promised Messiah. This causes Elizabeth to joyously exclaim, "Behold, when the sound of your greeting reached my ears, the baby leaped in my womb for joy" (Luke 1:44).

We should be careful not to overemphasize the area of prenatal awareness, for our knowledge of it is still very sketchy. My desire is simply to point to the wonder of it all, and to suggest that for the healing of memories, in some instances, we may have to deal with factors that precede birth. God informed the youthful Jeremiah about his prenatal call, "Before I formed you in the womb I knew you, and before you were born I consecrated you" (Jeremiah 1:5). By this reminder, God reinforced Jeremiah's call and commissioning as a prophet. Surely the same God who used this remarkable power for good is able to heal the scars and hurts of painful memories, however far back they may go.

As overwhelming as is the mystery of human memory, there is one aspect of the divine memory which is still more incredible. It is Jeremiah who most clearly tells us about it. "I will forgive their iniquity, and their sin I will remember no more" (31:34). How can an omniscient God not remember something? This verse is found in a passage about the New Covenant, which we now know includes the Cross and all that God in Christ has done to wipe out our sins. Perhaps God Himself has had some kind of healing of memories so that, wonder of wonders, when He forgives, He really does forget as well. Certainly, we are in the presence of great mystery. Mystery leads to wonder, and wonder leads to praise!

2
WHAT IS HEALING OF MEMORIES?

UNFORTUNATELY, the phrase *healing of memories* has come to have various meanings. In the minds of many Christians today, it is a kind of quickie cure-all, a short-cut to emotional and spiritual maturity. Because emotional healing has, at times, been carried to extremes, some people have abandoned it altogether, calling it unscriptural and even unhealthy. I can certainly understand their fears. My own experience in this realm has taught me that there is no area where the wheat and the tares are more closely sown together than in psychology. Being the infant science that it is, it is filled with all sorts of newly emerging theories and approaches. It is only quite recently that the insights and proven truths of psychology are being integrated with a truly Christian approach to counseling. It is important to recognize that all truth is God's truth, whether it be at the Lord's table or in the laboratory test tube. We keep our balance by continually running all truths through the sieve of God's Word.

Healing of memories is a form of Christian counseling and prayer which focuses the healing power of the Spirit on certain types of emotional/spiritual problems. It is *one* and *only one* of such ministries; and should never be made the *one and only* form, for such overemphasis leads to exaggeration and misuse. It is very important that Christian workers possess both sufficient knowledge and Spirit-sensitized discernment to know when it is the right tool of the Spirit for healing. One of the main purposes of this book is to help counselors and other Christian workers know when to use it and when not to use it.

In the usual course of memory healing, there are three phases. They are not always distinct and sometimes blend together. However, to help us clarify, we will look at them separately.

A Time of Counseling

God may use another person or a group to bring about the insights we have been unable to discover on our own. Counseling is often necessary to uncover the hidden hurts, the unmet needs, and the repressed emotions which are preventing us from getting to the truth which will set us free. In many instances, there can be no true healing and spiritual growth until we are released from painful memories and unhealthy patterns which now interfere with our present attitudes and behavior.

When I answered my office phone one afternoon, a man's anxious voice plunged me right into the situation— "We've got marriage problems," he said a bit curtly. "Can I send my wife to see you?" I usually find appointments by proxy do not work out too well. Soon a feminine voice on another line assured me she had asked her husband to take the initiative. Within a few days, I was listening to Patty tell me about a faltering marriage, a new lack of affection for her minister husband, and a whole spectrum of physical and emotional difficulties which had obviously driven her to the brink of breakdown. I also sensed a deep commitment to God and to her marriage. Patty's childhood story sounded like a textbook case for healing of memories—a broken home, several instances of sexual abuse by family members, family illness and poverty which overloaded her with work and responsibility at an early age. It was as if a Pandora's box full of painful memories had suddenly flown open to cause her present defeat.

However, when we went over the details of her scarred and sordid childhood, I was deeply impressed with the mature way she had handled it all. Sexual traumas and painful experiences had not kept her from being feminine in her outlook and completely normal in her responses to her husband. Her early experiences, painful as they had been, had actually helped make her a better mother to her children. In the end, it became clear she did not need a healing of those hurts from her past. An early teenage conversion and a loving church had enabled her to make peace with them rather remarkably.

We discovered that the real problem was a deep-seated bitterness she had allowed to take root in her heart a couple of years before. You see, her husband had felt the call to preach late in life. This meant leaving a lucrative position, thus forcing certain economic sacrifices upon Patty. Certainly this had reactivated her early fears of being poor and had added intensity to her resentments; but the crux of her difficulty was her more up-to-date feeling toward her husband. Gradually she had allowed this to affect her actions, so that she had been walling him out of her life and blaming him for other unrelated matters. This had blocked the flow of their hitherto healthy love life so that the whole relationship was breaking down. She had to face the ugliness of her sinful resentment and the subtle ways in which she had been getting even with him. In confession and prayer, she found grace to forgive him and to accept forgiveness for her wrong attitude and her hurtful actions. When they communicated all this to one another, God's love was able to wash away the barriers and restore deep love on both sides.

I have deliberately chosen an illustration where counseling revealed that a healing of memories was *not* necessary, to point out the need for personal counseling. It is often difficult to determine whether healing of memories is called for, and it is at this point that I have many reservations about using this form of emotional/spiritual healing with large groups of people or in mass meetings. Some clergy attempt this, and I surely would not limit God's power. I know that He uses sermons on inner healing to reveal to us our needs, and this is, in a sense, mass counseling. I have also seen some wonderful miracles of healing that had their beginnings in this kind of a public service. But I have strong reservations about trying to lead a whole audience through this process. Like much that takes place in the field of healing today, it is more magic than miracle. It's very rare to see long-term and lasting results, with permanent changes in attitudes and relationships, apart from a process that includes all three of the phases about which we are writing. The first is opening up to a counselor, pastor, or trusted friend. "Confess your faults to one another and pray for one another, so that you may be healed" (James 5:16).

A Time of Special Healing Prayer

This is one of the distinctives about the healing of memories. So that the Holy Spirit may actually touch the barriers to health, a full use is made of conversational prayer with emphasis on visualization, imagination, the pinpointing in time of the specific situation which produced the painful memory, and a deeply empathetic faith on the part of the praying partner.

In this special prayer, we allow the Spirit to take us back in time to the actual experience and to walk through those painful memories with us. It is then, through the use of our sanctified imaginations, that we pray as if we were actually there at the time it took place, allowing God to minister to us in the manner we needed at that time.

This prayer time is the very heart of the healing of memories. It is in prayer that the healing miracle begins; without it, the whole process may simply be a form of autosuggestion, catharsis, or feeling therapy. This special time of prayer cannot be bypassed, if there are to be lasting results.

At times we do not receive what we pray for, because we ask for the wrong things and from the wrong motives (James 4:2-3). It is important that our praying be on target. One of the miracles which often takes place during this special prayer time is that *the Holy Spirit becomes our Counselor who clarifies the content and purifies the motives of the prayer itself.* Often we begin by praying about the memory of a particular incident, or about a particular relationship, because we have thought one of those was the heart of the problem. Then, during the time of prayer, the Spirit peels away that layer and opens us up to deeper levels of our own minds and helps us *to discover what the real issue is.* This is extremely important and later we shall spend a lot of time on it. Because of our fallenness and the sinful responses we make to people who hurt us, we often develop very selective memories. That is, our recall of some things can become distorted because of the intensity of the emotions connected with them. Do you remember our description in chapter 1 of the junctions or *synapses* which pass along the electro-chemical impulses and thus send information to the brain? There are hundreds of these in which *information can be altered before, during, or after it has been received.* (See *Our Fragile Brains,* D. Gareth Jones, InterVarsity Press, pp. 43-44.)

Our attitudes of mind, emotion, and spirit play a big part in memory processing and can often throw us clear off the track when it comes to finding out insights necessary for healing. This is why Jesus' words about truth are so essential, "You shall know the truth, and the truth shall make you free" (John 8:32) His favorite name for the Holy Spirit was "The Spirit of Truth" (John 14—16). Sometimes, after we have gone as far as we can through counseling, it is during this time of prayer when the Spirit of Truth focuses like a great laser beam on the real need and brings His healing light to bear upon it.

Jack was a young man in his thirties, single, attractive, and with a good job. Recently he had been having bouts with depression. Although he had been a Christian for many years, he was filled with a generalized guilt which made it difficult for him to believe that God really loved him. He described his feelings this way: "There are invisible chains around me; I keep asking God to break them, but feel He won't do it—not for *me.* I have a sense of hopelessness, unworthiness." He shared with me his obvious abilities in art and music: "People tell me I have a lot of talents. I'd like to use them for the Lord, but I get all tied up in knots and can't express them. So I get angry at myself and feel that God is disappointed in me too."

At work he had difficulty standing up for his proper rights; as a result, his boss and coworkers took unfair advantage of him. They even told him they did. Why did he allow this? "I'm afraid I will be rejected even more than I *was*." I noticed the past tense and asked what that meant. In the next few sessions, he shared with me the picture of a home filled with constant rejection, put-down, and even physical abuse. Some of his worst memories were awakening from a night's sleep because his father was yelling at him and hitting him. This often occurred a few hours after a bedtime routine, when he would have to make up a story about his own wrongdoings, to satisfy his father's insistent accusations! His mother had "spells" when she would scream and throw things, breaking valuable belongings. The home was an atmosphere of utter unpredictability.

During our conversations, most of his feelings seemed to be directed against his parents. He casually mentioned an older sister, but only in passing. However, during the healing prayer time everything changed, and a great river of rage erupted against the sister. She somehow had a very unique and privileged position in this irrational family, and on scores of occasions could have protected and saved Jack from a great deal of suffering. Instead, she had increased it. Whenever she introduced him to her friends she would say sarcastically, "Don't pay attention to anything Jack does—he's mentally retarded." She actually added her suspicions to those of his parents and made his position worse. After they had both left home, Jack talked to her once about the fact that they were never shown any physical affection. He was deeply hurt when, instead of giving any understanding or comfort, she said angrily, "What'd you want me to do about it, hug you?"

When the Holy Spirit began to translate some of the
deep sighs and groanings which came out of the pit of his
painful memories (Romans 8:26-27), it became obvious
that this was the place Jack needed the deepest healing.
He had by far the greatest struggle in forgiving his sister,
not his parents. It was only after a long time of wrestling
with his resentments, and allowing the Spirit to "tear
them from his heart like a bunch of leeches," that he
forgave her and in turn received God's forgiveness for his
years of hidden bitterness. And it was all the result of the
prayer time. After all, the Holy Spirit is the true Counsel-
or who leads us into all truth.

Whether or not the prayer time is an occasion of new
perceptions, it is always a time of new power. And this
power is what saves the healing of memories from being
just another form of therapy in which people "psych
themselves out" and "feel good." The prayer time is when
the probing power of God Himself penetrates into the
deepest levels of our personalities. Hundreds of times I
have had people say to me afterward, "I really
wondered . . . I felt changed and different but I was skeptical. Would it last? Would my attitude be different when
I actually had to face the offending person or be back in
the situation? Well, I found out that I really had been
healed. God did it, and as I look back, I realize it all
happened while we were praying together." And this usually leads to a prayer of thanksgiving and praise.

A Time of Follow-up
The painful memories need to be integrated into life and
invested with new meaning. During this time the counselee, the counselor, and the Holy Spirit work together to
reprogram wrong attitudes and behavior patterns so as to

insure permanent changes. The ultimate goal here is not simply relief from the pain of the past or some level of mental and emotional health, but a growth in Christlikeness and a maturing work of sanctification and true holiness. Then the "healed helper" will be able to actually use his or her painful memories as an instrument of blessing in the lives of others.

Sometimes this follow-up requires a great deal of hard work, for *the healing of memories does not automatically computerize us into perfect performance and guarantee different behavior.* The real tragedy of hurtful memories is not simply the intense pain we feel from them and the powerful push from the past they stir up inside us. *It is that because of the pain and the push we have learned wrong ways of coping with life situations and wrong ways of relating to people, until these have become the basis of our personality patterns—our way of life.* These patterns must be changed by the sanctifying power of the Spirit working through our daily disciplines. The difference now is that we can be freed from the pains and the pushes and the compulsions.

3
WHY DO SOME MEMORIES NEED HEALING?

///////////

AN UNKNOWN AUTHOR has said, "Memory is the power to gather roses in winter." Obviously, this refers to the joyous aspect of good memories. Proverbs 10:7 comments on this, "The memory of the righteous is blessed." Paul wrote to the Philippians, "I thank my God every time I remember you" (1:3, NIV). Truly happy memories like these were Paul's roses in winter. They brought color and warmth to the damp and desolate atmosphere of the Roman jail where Paul was a prisoner when he wrote the letter.

I once conducted a service for some emotionally disturbed people in a Kentucky hospital. Many of them had come from the mountains in the eastern section of the state. The chaplain had shared with me some of their backgrounds—poverty, unemployment, a high incidence of child abuse, alcoholism, and family tragedy. In my

message I talked about God's grace which could comfort
them and heal the emotional wounds which had been a
factor in producing their breakdowns. To close the service, the chaplain gave them the opportunity of choosing
a favorite hymn. I was surprised when several selected the
well-known Appalachian Gospel song, "Precious Memories, How They Linger." In the midst of their overwhelming mental pain, they were making every effort to
remember only the roses of their past. But their physical
and emotional conditions were living proof that they had
refused to face up to or make peace with their many
thorns.

Time Heals All Wounds—Or Does It?

It's time that we take a closer look at one of the great
myths about healing—that time heals all wounds. The
falseness is in the word *all*. True, there are many wounds
which time by itself can heal. If the mind can consciously
endure the pain when it is being experienced, then, as
time passes, the intensity of the painful memory will less-
en. With sufficient time, only the memory of having suffered will remain. There will still be pain in the memory,
but it will be bearable. It will be somewhat like a successful operation which does not develop infection. It can
certainly be very painful, but it will gradually heal without complication. Someday only a sensitive scar will
remind us of the suffering we went through. *Yes, time can
heal all unrepressed and uninfected painful memories.*

But time by itself does not and cannot heal those memories which are so painful that the person's mind cannot
tolerate them. The evidence shows that such experiences
are as alive and as painful ten or twenty years later as they
were ten or twenty minutes after they were pushed out of

consciousness. What cannot be faced and borne is denied. Let us use an extreme illustration, to show how wonderfully God has provided us with a built-in protection system for one of His most precious gifts to us—our minds.

People in serious automobile accidents almost never remember the actual moment of impact. That final experience of binding and searing pain is rarely, if ever, within recall. They often remember many things just prior to that moment. They will say, "I could see that we were going to hit that bridge," or "I remember the truck bearing down on us," or "I can see in my mind when we started over the cliff." But they do not remember the experience of going through the windshield, or when they were thrown out of the car, or actually hitting the abutment. Thank God they don't! Can you imagine what it would be like to go through life with that kind of a mental picture permanently stored in the memory? Such a person would not be able to maintain sanity. He could not bear the overwhelming emotional pain which would accompany such a memory. So God in His mercy has provided a kind of mental and emotional fuse which simply blows itself when the circuits get overloaded.

This illustration contains both the physical and emotional factors which make it easy for us to understand *how* and *why* the fuse blows. Mental pain can produce similar results. I shall never forget the sad and bewildered face of a Korean War veteran who was shown on TV many years ago. His painful battle and prisoner-of-war experiences had left him without any identification tags and with almost complete amnesia. He couldn't even remember his own name and personal identity. We all ached for him as he looked out through our TV screens and asked, "Can anyone tell me who I am?" Fortunately, for him and many others, the memories were restored.

Repressed Memories

Sometimes serious crimes are solved when long-forgotten events are recalled that provide important clues. The Associated Press carried the following story in our local newspaper on December 21, 1979 (*The Lexington Herald*, Lexington, Kentucky):

WOMAN'S MIND UNLOCKS CLUE TO DAD'S MURDER 35 YEARS AGO

RAEFORD, N.C. - Edward Leon Cameron disappeared 35 years ago. Sheriff Dave Barrington went looking for him last week and turned up a bizarre murder locked since childhood in a woman's mind.

For years Mrs. Perry had not been aware that something grotesque, too horrible to think about, was suppressed in her memory. But, according to Barrington, it resurfaced during (treatment). . . .

It was April 8, 1944, and Annie Blue Cameron was just short of her 10th birthday. That night, she now remembers, she overheard her parents quarreling in the family's farmhouse.

The next day, she "opened the door to the front bedroom and saw her father's body on the floor. . . . He appeared to be dead," reads a search warrant drawn up last week. "The next week after school, (she) went to the outhouse. She looked down the hole and saw her father's face barely submerged under the excrement."

But those events were frozen in the minds of a little girl and her mother, Winnie Cameron, who gave up her terrible knowledge only in death.

Barrington said the story began to unfold after
Mrs. Perry sought psychiatric help. . . . Mrs.
Perry had been unwilling to discuss the case
with anyone but the authorities, and the nature
of her psychological problems has not been
discussed.

Mrs. Perry, now a reading teacher at Valencia
Community College in Orlando, Florida, eventually got in touch with the FBI. And last
Christmas she confronted her mother in a telephone call, taped by the authorities with her
permission.

"Ma, I feel like you had something to do with
my father's death," said Mrs. Perry, according to
the sheriff. Mrs. Cameron refused to discuss it,
he said.

On December 1 of this year, Mrs. Perry called
her mother again. "I want to talk to you again
about what I discussed last Christmas," she said.
"Is my father's body still in that toilet?"

Her mother replied, "I will tell you after
Christmas."

The digging started December 12. Mrs. Perry
and her sister, June Ivey, helped law officers
locate the place where the outhouse had stood.

"At 1:20 P.M., we hit the remains. . . . It
was a rib," Barrington said. "After that it was
just bone after bone all afternoon." Only
Cameron's skull and a few other bones remain
unearthed.

"Mrs. Cameron was in the house most of the
day (Dec. 12)," Barrington said. "She only left
the next morning at 8 A.M. That was the last
time she was seen by my department alive."

Late Friday afternoon, the Cameron son . . .
found Mrs. Cameron, 69, lying beside her car
on a back boundary of the family's farmland, a
.32-caliber pistol clutched in her hand. On the
car seat lay an envelope. . . . Barrington (said)
it contained a confession.

Some time ago I was giving a seminar at the Duke
University School of Medicine Department of Psychiatry
and mentioned this incident. A young resident told me
he was from the very town where all this had happened
and vouched for the truthfulness of the facts in the newspaper article.

This incident illustrates one of the mysteries of memory—the ability to block out of our minds things which
we are not able to face. The saddest part of this is that
though we may block out the pain quite *unintentionally*,
we still suffer the consequences. Often, as in the case of
Mrs. Perry, it's not until those memories literally explode
and begin to affect our daily lives that we are forced to do
something about them.

Many of us have hurtful memories which we try to push
out of our minds. Such memories cannot be healed by the
mere passage of time any more than an infected wound
could be. The infection turns inward and actually worsens
because it spreads to other areas, affecting and infecting
them. So it is with certain painful experiences, especially
those that happen during the important years of early
childhood and teenage development. In severe situations,
a dissociation or splitting off and storing away of the experience can take place. It then seems to be deposited
into a part of the memory which is not immediately available to conscious recall. No one completely understands
the mental, emotional, and neurological process. But we

do know that it requires a great deal of continuous emotional and spiritual energy to keep the memory in its hidden place.

It could be compared to a person trying to hold a bunch of balloons under water. He succeeds for a while but finally runs out of energy; then they pop up here and there, in spite of his desperate efforts. Such repressed and fixated memories can never really be forgotten. Nor can they simply be filed away in the same way our minds store pleasant memories, with their accompanying good feelings. For the harder we try to keep bad memories out of conscious recall, the more powerful they become. Since they are not allowed to enter through the door of our minds directly, they come into our personalities (body, mind, and spirit) in disguised and destructive ways. These denied problems go underwater and later reappear as certain kinds of physical illnesses, unhappy marital situations, and recurring cycles of spiritual defeat.

As I was writing this chapter, I was interrupted by a long-distance call from another state. A man had read *Healing for Damaged Emotions* a few weeks before and wanted to talk with me. He had been a Christian for over seven years, faithful in his Bible reading, prayer life, and fellowship with other believers. But there were areas of life where, as he said, "The needle seemed stuck in repetitive emotional patterns." He went on to say that although he had tried every Christian discipline he knew, he simply could not figure out what the problem was. While reading the book, he felt as if the Holy Spirit had stripped off a layer of his memory so that he could remember some things which were related to his "broken record" problems. There was no particular trauma; rather, it was a whole atmosphere, an environment with a pervading tone he had absorbed while growing up. And though he hated it, he discovered he was *unintentionally* trying to reproduce that very same climate in his present relationships. He kept stressing the fact he had not realized what he was doing *until he remembered.* Now that he understood, he was able to share the memories with a counselor and receive even deeper insights. And through praying with his wife, he was seeing changes in himself and in his home atmosphere. I hung up the phone thanking God for an up-to-date confirmation of the effects of buried memories.

The man's story is also a needed balance to some of the more extreme illustrations I have used. For often, we are not able to pinpoint particular experiences or happenings. Instead, as with this man, it can be an aggregate of surrounding influences, an all-pervasive atmosphere which encompasses us with *a whole set of generalized memories which require healing.* I'm sure this is a part of what Jesus had in mind when He spoke of the destructive effects of some actions upon children, and then uttered one of His most severe judgments upon those who "offend these little ones" or "cause them to stumble" (Matthew 18:6-7 and Luke 17:1-3). Truly, "it would be better for him if a millstone were hung around his neck and he were thrown into the sea."

Creating Trust Conditions for Conscious Recall

People who carry hurtful memories will allow them to come into conscious recall (remembrance) only under certain *trust conditions.* This is why an understanding and empathetic counselor is often needed, someone whom the hurting person can trust and who can lead him or her into the presence of a caring and trustworthy God. In fact, it is precisely at this point that the Gospel is truly good news—the incredible news of the understanding and saving companionship of God Himself. Christ's sufferings on the Cross *for* us and *as* us provide the *trust conditions* which enable the sufferer to bring those painful memories into the light of consciousness so they can not only be faced but healed.

The creation of these trust conditions needs to begin with the way we present the Gospel and in the very atmosphere of our churches.

4
CREATING THE ATMOSPHERE FOR HEALING

/////////////

AT THE END of World War II, the Japanese government was faced with a massive problem. Even though the peace documents had been signed, there were thousands of Japanese soldiers in the mountains and jungles of South Pacific islands who would not come out of hiding, surrender their arms, and return to a life of peace. They had been so thoroughly brainwashed by their officers with stories of what the Americans would do to them if they gave themselves up that they fully believed surrender would mean either torture or instant death. Finally, the Japanese Emperor made a speech explaining the situation and pleading with his men to come home. The speech was broadcast by radio and also recorded and repeatedly boomed toward the mountain caves and the jungles by loudspeaker. In essence he said to them, "Come out, the war is over. Peace has been established. You will not be harmed, but wel-

43

comed and protected."

Since it was the voice of their Emperor himself, almost all of the troops accepted his assurance and came out. There were stragglers, of course, but within months all but a few had surrendered. After some years, it was assumed that all the living had been accounted for. However, it was not until March of 1974 that the last soldier finally came out of hiding, twenty-nine years after the war was over! By now the two countries were on friendly terms. When they asked the man, now in his sixties, why he had waited, he said it had taken him that long to get over his fears.

In chapter 3, we said we allow certain kinds of painful memories to come into conscious recollection or remembrance only under the right kind of trust conditions. Without those conditions we are like the old Japanese soldier. Our fears will not, cannot, allow us to lower our defenses so that our buried memories can come out of hiding. In a very real sense, God, the loving Heavenly Father, the Emperor of the Universe, has sent us all His special message of peace. Perhaps it is best expressed by Paul, in 2 Corinthians 5:19, "God was in Christ reconciling the world to Himself, not counting their trespasses against them." Here is the very heart of the Good News—"Come out, you don't need to be afraid any longer. There is peace between us. You will not be harmed or punished, but welcomed and accepted."

Why is it, then, that so many people do *not* feel free to open themselves up to the healing grace of God? Why are they still hiding behind all manner of defenses? *The reason is that all too often the atmosphere in our churches, the attitudes of other Christians, and the very way we proclaim the Gospel do not create the trust conditions which are necessary for healing.*

The Pastor as Prophet and Priest

There are different functions of preaching, different kinds of sermons, and different goals at which they are aimed. Many sermons represent the *prophetic role* of the messenger. He stands as God's representative and proclaims God's Word, "Thus saith the Lord." As prophet he should, like Jesus, speak with authority. In this role the minister's aim is to proclaim truth, expound the great doctrines of the faith, and uphold biblical standards for ethical living. As prophet he speaks of sin, righteousness, and judgment, and calls people to repentance, salvation, sanctification, and holiness of heart and life.

When he preaches in his *priestly or pastoral role*, the content and the aim are different. As God's representative he offers the nourishment of the Word, building up and encouraging the people. He brings comfort to the sorrowing and hope to those in despair. In the words of Charles Wesley's beautiful hymn, "Jesus, Lover of My Soul," the pastor's aim in this kind of preaching is to "raise the fallen, cheer the faint, heal the sick, and lead the blind."

Most of our preaching falls somewhere between the prophetic and the pastoral approach. Indeed, to be what God intended preaching to be, there should be a balance between the two aspects of the Gospel—moral demand and gracious gift. Of course, our Lord Himself combined the two most perfectly, as in His words to the woman taken in adultery, "Neither do I condemn thee; go, and sin no more" (John 8:11, KJV). Most ministers try their best to be faithful to both emphases and generally are able to meet the needs of most of their listeners. What they often fail to recognize is the increasingly large number of people in their congregations who need to be reached by an even deeper level of preaching. Edgar N. Jackson, in his book, *A Psychology for Preaching*, reports on a questionnaire given to 4,000 people. Its purpose was to find out what people want from their pastors through sermons. Half of them expressed a concern about intensely personal matters—the futility of life, insecurity in personal relationships, loneliness, marital problems, the control of their sexual desires, the effects of alcohol, false ideas of religion and morals, feelings of inferiority, the problems of illness and suffering, and feelings of guilt and frustration. Another fourth were chiefly concerned with family problems, parenthood, childrearing, and relational conflict. The remaining fourth were concerned with the more traditional religious problems (Harper and Row, pp. 75-77).

Here is a cry for help which needs to be heard and answered through our evangelical preaching. A lot of spiritual needs arise out of immaturity, inner conflict, emotional and relational hangups. People want to know how to live this abundant life we are always preaching about, in the nitty-gritty of daily living.

To these normal human problems we in North America must add a whole list of abnormal ones. Truly, we have sown to the wind and are reaping the whirlwind, as an increasing number of people, including many born-again and Spirit-filled Christians, are coming into young adulthood with serious emotional problems which deeply affect their spiritual lives. In our increasingly sick society, the situation seems to grow worse by geometric proportion, like a population explosion.

Our tragic overemphasis on sex has become almost a national obsession:
- the explosive rise of divorce in the last four decades,
- the alarming increase in child and spouse abuse, incest and sexual violation,
- the growing addiction to liquor and drugs,

• the breakdown of moral standards, discipline, and the sense of responsibility.

All of these have helped make our society an assembly line for turning out disturbed people with damaged emotions. And many of these damaged emotions are deeply buried in layers of memory which will not respond to the kind of preaching we ordinarily hear. In fact, we can say some of our traditional preaching actually causes such people greater fear and hardens their defenses so that those memories are driven still further underground. Even in sermons of comfort or encouragement, it is possible to present the Good News in such a way as to deepen people's despair. Many times when I ask people why they don't share their problems with their pastor they tell me it is because they already know what he will say. He will simply make them feel guiltier than they already do. When I pursue this further by asking them how they know this, they usually reply, "I can tell by the way he preaches." It would be easy for evangelists and pastors to dismiss this judgment as unfair. The fact is that it hurts because it is so often true. *Too often our preaching discourages people even more and deters them from seeking the help and healing they so desperately need.*

Preaching for Emotional and Spiritual Healing

Years of experience in this area have taught me that a special kind of preaching is needed to encourage a healing of memories. It is distinctive in its content, style, and aim. The task of this type of preaching is:

• to give the sufferer the courage to lower the defenses which have prevented his healing,

• to enable him to bring out into the open his buried inner fears, anxieties, conflicts, and shame,

• to help him exteriorize his hidden and deeply internalized memories in the presence of the Cross,

• to create what is, perhaps, to him a completely new image of God, an empathetic Father who is not shocked but understanding of whatever is uncovered in His presence, because He has known about it all along and has never stopped loving.

The Content of the Preaching

The heart of this special kind of sermon is found in certain fundamental aspects of the Good News we have in Christ.

• Incarnation—Emmanuel, God is with us. The Apostle John wrote, "The Word was made flesh, and dwelt among us" (John 1:14, KJV). Matthew quoted Isaiah's prophecy, "Behold, a virgin shall be with child, and shall bring forth a Son, and they shall call His name Emmanuel, which being interpreted is, God with us" (Matthew 1:23, KJV).

Among us . . . With us. What does this mean that God is with us? When we think of how we use the word *with*, we get a clue. Sometimes we go to a friend who is suffering from disease, or pain, or great loss. We want to convey our deepest feelings of sympathy. So we say, "I want you to know that I am with you in this, with you all the way." This is a meaning of the Incarnation we need to convey. Isaiah prophesied about the coming of Emmanuel, and Matthew explained the meaning, "which being interpreted is, God with us." In our preaching to people suffering from mental and emotional pain, we need to speak of the real humanity of Christ. It is not that "the Word became words." Words are needed, but they are not enough, not even for God Himself. The Word became *flesh.* God has come down into the arena of human living and suffering. *He has become one with us by becoming one of us.*

• Identification—God is in our pain with us. Perhaps I can best illustrate this point by telling two true stories which were reported in the Canadian newspaper, *The Calgary Herald.*

On June 5, 1978, seven-year-old Martin Turgeon slipped off the wharf and fell into the Prairie River. The dozen or more adults standing on the same pier did nothing—except watch him struggle a few moments in the water and then drown.

Why didn't anyone help? Well, just a short distance upstream, untreated sewage is dumped into the river. The water is highly polluted and very smelly. One witness quoted an onlooker as later saying, "We weren't going to jump in there—the water was much too dirty." A policeman who came on the scene shortly thereafter remarked bitterly, "It makes you wonder about how human people really are. The boy probably could have been saved."

Contrast that incident with this one. In August of 1977, John Everingham, an Australian journalist working in Laos, was expelled by the Communists. Engaged to marry a national of that land, Keo Sirisomhone, he was forced to leave her behind. For ten months John carefully planned how to rescue Keo. Finally, on May 27, 1978 he set out on his mission of rescue. Outfitted with face masks, fins, and a scuba diving tank equipped with two breathing devices, he plunged into the rain-swollen Mekong River which separates Laos from Thailand.

Because of the murky water, there was zero visibility below the surface, and John had to use a compass which was on his face mask. He battled swirling currents, crawling along the muddy bottom where he was occasionally tossed about by whirlpools. When he surfaced he discovered that he had underestimated the current. He was still several hundred feet off shore and being carried past the spot where Keo was waiting, disguised as a fisherwoman to avoid any suspicion. Exhausted, Everingham swam back to the Thai side.

This time he entered the river further upstream. Let me quote him at this point. "I made it, and crawled out on the bank. Keo seemed to have given up and was dejectedly walking away in the distance. I yelled at the top of my lungs. She turned and saw me and, running forward, fell into my arms." Keo had never learned to swim so John put a slightly inflated life vest around her neck and one of the breathing regulators in her mouth. With their faces just at the surface of the water and a quick-release strap binding them together, John pushed hard into the river. After a desperate struggle they made it together, falling exhausted on the bank on the other side—in Thailand!

John's story illustrates Emmanuel's identification with us in our terrible human predicament. He is not a God who stands by, unwilling to get involved, but a God who loves us so much that He is willing to plunge into the turbulent and murky waters of human life and be identified with us all the way:

• in His very conception, submerged in the amniotic fluids, the waters of the Virgin Mary's womb,

• in His birth and infancy, fleeing the swirling waters of King Herod's insane death decree,

• in His boyhood, learning through the waters of growth and development, maturing from the discipline of earthly parents and religious authorities,

• in His thirty years, immersed in the waters of obscurity, soaking in Scripture, being saturated in patience and divine wisdom,

• all through His life and ministry, plunging into the polluted waters of sin-corrupted lives, baptized with sinners, eating with them, and risking their contamination,

• and finally, engulfed in the whirlpools of deceit, denial, and betrayal, entering the murky depths of death itself . . . even the death of the Cross.

• Crucifixion—God is in our pain with us and for us, all the way, even at great cost to Himself. Now we have reached the very core of the Good News—the Cross. Jesus identified with the worst of us right to the end, as He was crucified with two criminals. Here in the deepest waters of all, "He suffered death, so that by the grace of God He might taste death for everyone" (Hebrews 2:9, NIV).

This identification in death was crucially important, as the author of the Book of Hebrews tells us . . . "He too shared in their humanity so that by His death He might destroy him who holds the power of death—that is, the devil—and free those who all their lives were held in slavery by their fear of death. . . . For this reason He had to be made like His brothers in every way. . . . Because He Himself suffered when He was tempted, He is able to help those who are being tempted" (Hebrews 2:14-18, NIV). Here is complete identification with us, the ultimate proof that God understands our pain and our suffering. The point of this passage and others from the Epistle to the Hebrews is that because God now fully understands, we never need hesitate to bring anything to Him. Indeed, we are urged to "approach the throne of grace with confidence, so that we may receive mercy and find grace to help us in our time of need" (Hebrews 4:16, NIV).

We do not really convey the meaning of this invitation if we limit the death of Christ to atonement for sins.

Certainly the Cross means that Christ died for our sins; but if we confine it to that, we are missing one element in our preaching and teaching which millions of hurting people need to hear. For by His Cross, Christ reconciles to God both sinners and sufferers. When Christ descended into hell, He not only brought cleansing from the guilty memories of our sins which condemn our consciences; He also brought healing for those painful memories which arise within us to torment and enslave our personalities. Many of these memories come from injuries and infirmities which we did not choose. Rather, we were victims of the sinful choices of others. And that is exactly what Christ allowed Himself to be on the Cross—a victim of the choices of others. As He voluntarily subjected Himself to the ultimate penalty for our sins, He went through the most painful experience of human life—undeserved and unjust suffering. He deliberately submitted Himself to the twin mysteries of sin and suffering. Our preaching is much too simplistic if we limit the Atonement to the forgiveness of sins.

There are those who would immediately ask, "Whose sins?" In the passage from Matthew regarding sins against children, which we quoted in chapter 3, Jesus went on to say, "Woe to the world because of the things that cause people to sin! Such things must come, but woe to the man through whom they come!" (Matthew 18:7, NIV) Yes, we have all sinned and need the forgiveness which the Cross provides. But because we are also sinned against, we need assurance from the Cross that God understands the complicated and contradictory emotions we experience, the inner hell of tangled feelings which erupt from unhealed memories.

One of the angriest moments in my counseling ministry was while I was listening to a sobbing young lady unfold her story. Judy had heard a well-known evangelist preach and had gone to him for prayer and guidance. In great agony she shared with him how her minister father had repeatedly molested her sexually, beginning at the age of six. She confessed her confused feelings which constantly kept her depressed and spiritually defeated—a jumbled mixture of guilt, shame, sexual ambivalence, anger, and sadness. His immediate reply was that if she would "repent" for her part in all this, God would "straighten out" her feelings. He faithfully expounded the "plan of salvation." He was so full of answers that he did not even take time to listen to her questions or to hear the full story, which included the fact that her mother, in a fit of rage, had broken Judy's leg when she was only three years old.

The miracle of God's grace is such that, in spite of the sickness of her home, this young lady was a genuine Christian. She had indeed experienced forgiveness and the new birth in Christ. What she desperately needed was to be healed from the sordid scars of the past and to learn a whole new way of relating to God, others, and herself.

This is why the preaching of the Cross in its fullest sense is so central to create the trust conditions necessary for the healing of memories. How beautifully the ancient Communion liturgy puts it: "Through faith in His blood" we receive "the remission of our sins," and "all other benefits of His passion." Let us be sure that our version of the Good News includes this benefit which so many wounded spirits need. In His first sermon in the synagogue, as recorded by Luke, Jesus' proclamation of the Good News included the description of the Messiah from Isaiah 61:1-2. "He has sent Me to bind up the brokenhearted, to proclaim freedom for the captives." Surely the brokenhearted of our churches need to know that He has borne their griefs and infirmities, as well as their sins.

• Living Reality—of an empathetic and understanding God. What does all this mean? How does it affect our daily lives? And how does it create the atmosphere for the healing we have been talking about? It changes our concepts and feelings about God and thus produces a climate of trust in which deeply submerged memories can emerge.

Why is this true? Because God now knows how we humans feel. Yes, God has always known this, because God is God and knows all things. So how can we say God *now* knows? That seems to mean that He has learned something new, and this would make Him less than perfect, thus less than God. In the sense that God is omniscient, He has always known; but now, *He actually knows* from experience. Those wonderful passages in Hebrews imply there is a deeper sense in which God now *knows and understands* because of the sufferings of Christ. I hesitate to use a very personal illustration, but it's the only one I know that can explain what I mean.

Prior to our going to India, Helen and I spent a year of study in a missionary training school, where we had a valuable course in Tropical Medicine. One of the facts we learned was that fifty percent of all babies in India die before the age of five. We knew the fact of infant mortality. But two years later when our ten-month-old son, David, died within a few hours after an attack of fulminant bacillary dysentary, and we buried him that March morning in the red soil of Bidar, India, Helen and I came to know about infant mortality in a new way.

Of course, God understood what it meant to be a human being. But because of the Incarnation, His ultimate identification with us in the sufferings and death of Christ, God now fully knows and understands, not simply from factual omniscience but from actual experience

Now we are sure that He knows and cares. Because He

has been one of us, because He has lived out our life at every point, from a human womb to a human tomb, we know He is "touched with the feeling of our infirmities" (Hebrews 4:15, KJV). And because we are sure that He *knows,* life need never be the same for us.

• Participation by His Spirit in our Healing. An empathetic, understanding God who knows and cares is the most therapeutic factor in our inner healing. But in a sense, all we have said is past tense—it is the Jesus of history. Thank God He has not left us there. The Jesus of history becomes the Christ of present and personal experience through the work of His Holy Spirit. It is the Spirit who takes all that He made *possible* by His sufferings, death, and resurrection and makes it *actual* in our lives now. The Holy Spirit is the *paraklete. Para*—alongside, and *kaleo*—to call. The One Called Alongside. And Romans 8:26-27 assures us that the Holy Spirit helps us with our infirmities, our cripplings, and our weaknesses. The Greek word for *help* is a compound of three words meaning "to take hold of on the other side." It is a beautiful and sensitive picture of the knowing, understanding, caring God who is now participating with us in our healing.

This assurance is set in the context of Romans 8:18-28, where Paul is talking about the pain and suffering of living in this fallen and imperfect world. Even the created world of nature "has been groaning as in the pains of childbirth right up to the present time." Yes, it is truly a hurting world. Then Paul goes on, "Not only so, but we ourselves, who have the firstfruits of the Spirit, groan inwardly as we wait eagerly for our adoption as sons, the redemption of our bodies." Yes, the world of nature groans and, although we are Christians, we too groan. But we are not left alone. *God Himself, in the presence of His Holy Spirit, also groans with us.* "In the same way, the Spirit helps us in our weakness. We do not know what we ought to pray, but the Spirit Himself intercedes for us with groans that words cannot express" (vv. 22-23, 26, NIV).

This must be at the heart of our preparatory preaching, this incredibly Good News which for many of our suffering hearers seems too good to be true. We must preach it with all the love and empathy and understanding we can receive from the Spirit, always sharing openly from our own lives where we have experienced this kind of inner healing and understanding love.

Redemptive Acceptance in the Congregation

In addition to the content of the preaching, there is another supremely important aspect for creating trust conditions. The pastor may preach the kind of sermons we have been describing. However, unless the attitudes of Christians in his church radiate the same kind of redemptive acceptance, there will not be the necessary climate for healing. Most of the fears and anxieties which keep people from opening up are caused by *pain from unhealthy interpersonal relationships.* As we have already seen, the memories of those relationships go far back in their lives, perhaps even before birth. These people learned a whole language of harmful relationships even before they learned to speak. It is essential that they now learn a new language of helpful relationships. But to learn it, they must first hear it spoken. That is why the people who make up the church play such an important part in the healing process. Supportive Christians need to surround struggling and suffering persons with an atmosphere of understanding and love. Sometimes in the name of love they may have to confront, but this will always be done in a spirit of restoration rather than judgment. If it has to be *tough* love, it will still be tough *love*.

Can we honestly say this is the kind of atmosphere we find in most of our churches? Christian businessman, speaker, and writer, Fred Smith, of Dallas, Texas has written an incisive modern parable on this theme. With his permission I am quoting much of it:

"DON'T TAKE ME TO THE HOSPITAL—PLEASE"

This scene didn't make sense. There he lay in the street bleeding; the hit-and-run driver gone. He needed medical help immediately. Yet, he kept pleading, "Don't take me to the hospital, please."

Surprised, everyone asked, "Why?"

Pleadingly he answered, "Because I am on the staff at the hospital. It would be embarrassing for them to see me like this. They have never seen me bleeding and dirty. They always see me clean and healthy. Now I am a mess."

"But the hospital is for people like you. Can't we call an ambulance?"

"No, please don't. I took a pedestrian safety course, and the instructor would criticize me for getting hit."

"But who cares what the instructor thinks? You need attention."

"But there are other reasons too—the admissions clerk would be upset."

"Why?"

"Because she always gets upset if anyone for admittance doesn't have all the details she needs to fill out her records. I didn't see who hit

me, and I don't even know the make of car or
license number. She wouldn't understand. She
is a real stickler for records. Worse than that, I
haven't got my medical insurance card."

"What real difference would that make?"

"Well, if they didn't recognize me in this
mess, they wouldn't let me in. They won't admit anyone in my shape without an insurance
card. They must be sure it isn't going to cost the
institution. They protect the institution. Just
pull me over to the curb. I'll make it some way.
It's my fault I got hit. Why should the nurses
get their clean uniforms dirty with me? They
would criticize me."

With this he tried to crawl to the gutter while
everyone left him alone. Maybe he made it—
maybe he didn't. Maybe he is still trying to stop
his own bleeding.

Does that strike you as a strange, ridiculous
story? It could happen any Sunday . . . in a
typical church. I know it could happen because
last night I asked some active Christians what
they would do if Saturday night they got hit and
run over by some unacceptable sin. Without ex-
ception they said, "I sure wouldn't want to go to
church the next morning where everybody
would see me."

In the good-natured spirit of the conversation, we decided if caught—hit and run over by
sin—we would be better off to go to the pool
hall instead of the church. . . . There we would
find sympathy and understanding.

We kept exploring: Is the church for imita-
tion saints, dressed up and smelling good, or is

it for the bleeding who know they have been hit and run over and who want to get well? Somehow the question stops being one for the entire church as it becomes singularly mine—one individual—one sinner saved by grace—one human being striving to insulate myself in a superior group or becoming involved in the total need.

"Behold how they love one another." The winners and the losers, the healthy and the sick, the hurt and the well. I need to be a giver and receiver in a church where the hurt will say expectantly, "Take me to the church, please."

The healing of memories requires a corporate fellowship of believers as caring as the paralytic's four friends, who risked tearing up the roof in order to bring him into the presence of Jesus for healing. People will allow their most painful memories to come into conscious recollection (remembrance) and thus risk the possibility of healing only within _trust conditions._ You may be wondering just how we can achieve those conditions. I remind you that the Good News is Christ crucified and resurrected. Listen to John's account of what happened on that first Easter evening. "On the evening of that first day of the week, when the disciples were together, with the doors locked for fear of the Jews, Jesus came and stood among them and said, 'Peace be with you!' After He said that, He showed them His hands and side" (John 20:19, NIV). _The risen Christ came right through the doors which had been locked out of fear._

Praise God, our risen Lord can still walk right through the defenses and doors which have long been locked out of fear. He can still bring peace to pained and troubled hearts. He does it by _speaking words of peace_ and by *showing His scars*, the price He paid to bring us that peace. It's up to us, His disciples, to gather together in His name, in His Spirit, and create the atmosphere for His healing appearance.

5
BIBLICAL FOUNDATIONS FOR MEMORY HEALING

IT IS OF UTMOST IMPORTANCE to understand that the healing of memories has a solid foundation in the Scripture, which is our final authority in all matters of faith and practice. Some people have totally rejected all forms of inner healing because the precise definitions do not appear in the Bible. If we applied that reasoning to everything, we could be led to fanatical and even dangerous extremes—not wearing clothes with buttons; not driving cars; not using pianos, organs, or PA systems in church; refusing penicillin for a sick child and thus being the cause of his death. We would actually be denying that all truth comes from God and that we have a spiritual obligation to use every new insight and discovery in any area of life for God's glory and human good. The real question is not whether a practice appears in the Bible in the specific form or language we use today. Rather, the question is whether it is contradictory to or consistent with principles stated in Scripture. In accordance with this basic tenet, we Christians are grateful for all the new truths, insights, and discoveries which continually come to us from many fields such as medicine, sociology, mathematics, physics, and psychology. As we look at the biblical teachings, we find the principles upon which we base the healing of memories.

Put Away Childish Things

It is necessary to put away childish things in order to grow up spiritually. There are two different Greek words in the New Testament which refer to childhood. It is important that we keep them distinct.

Paidion is a word which refers to the time of childhood, in a healthy and normal sense. We get our words *pediatrics* and *pediatrician* from this root. *Paidion* is the word Jesus used when He brought a little child before the disciples and told them they needed to have the same qualities of humility and teachability as the child. He went so far as to tell them, "Unless you are converted and become like children, you shall not enter the kingdom of heaven" (Matthew 18:3). While we tend to tell children to grow up and become more like adults, Jesus was always telling adults to become more like children! Today, we would use the word *childlike* to express this idea. The Bible urges us to be more *childlike* in our faith, humility, acceptance, and openness to others. We are never to grow away from these *childlike* qualities.

The other word is *nepios*, which refers to childhood in an unhealthy and abnormal way, in the sense of remaining in a stage of protracted infancy and childhood when one should have grown beyond it. Nothing is more delightful than a child who acts like a child; and nothing is more dreadful than an adult who keeps on acting like a child. This kind of behavior can be downright disruptive and is sometimes destructive. Today we describe such a person as *childish*. If his behavior is extremely childish, we go further back to an even earlier stage of life and say *babyish*. *Nepios* is the word Paul used in Romans 2:20, Galatians 4:1, and 1 Corinthians 3:1 when he described people who were spiritually immature. In his great love chapter, 1 Corinthians 13, he wrote, "When I was a child, I spake as a child, I understood as a child, I thought as a child; but when I became a man, I put away childish things" (v. 11, KJV). Here he was referring to a combination of emotional and spiritual immaturity. Does this verse seem to be out of place in the middle of the great love chapter? It isn't at all, for the characteristics and behavior of *agape* love require a certain level of emotional and spiritual maturity. And that level can never be reached until we first put away childish things.

Paul's word for *put away* is the strong Greek word *katergeo*, which means "to render inoperative, inactive, or powerless; to remove the meaning and significance from; to free from that which has been keeping one bound or tied up." Maturity doesn't come simply because we grow older. We can be chronological grown-ups and psychological children at the same time. To be finished with childish things requires action by the person.

This biblical principle forms a fitting foundation for the fact that some people must undergo a healing of memories. Certain problems which prevent maturity we call *hangups*. We say people's hangups keep them *in a bind*. The words are amazingly accurate. When people have never faced their painful memories or been loosened (unbound) from them, they are still *hung up at a certain age and stage of their development.* Yes, their bodies are of adult size and their minds fully developed. But their emotions never grew past a certain level. At that particular point they got stuck, hung up; hence the term, personality or emotional hangups. Many of those hangups come as a result of memories which bind and hold us in a vicelike grip. Such painful memories are like weights tied to a swimmer's body. They keep pulling him down, so that he is just barely able to keep afloat, or they consume so much emotional and spiritual energy that he is not able to make any progress.

Phil and his wife, Janet, came to me for help after seeing a marriage counselor for several months. They loved each other very much and were both strongly committed to holding their marriage together. They expressed their willingness to work hard at it, and that's exactly what Phil had been doing. The main problem between them was that Phil could not express the deep love he felt for Janet, either in words or in physical affection. Of course, this affected their relationship in many areas. She was simply not receiving a normal share of emotional fulfillment and this made her irritable and impatient. He tried to compensate for his problem by being helpful around the house—in fact, he was too helpful and often got onto her turf. She interpreted this as interference and a put-down of her housekeeping. She said, "I appreciate his wanting to help, but it makes me feel as if he's not satisfied with the way I do things." And so there was set up a vicious circle of negative emotions which kept escalating.

The marriage counselor seemed to have only one approach: analyze the situation and see what the problems are. Then by prayer and effort, change the behaviors which are creating bad feelings. It is certainly a very sound approach and I have seen it work wonders in many situations. However, it is not the only one, for there are many people who are unable to change attitudes and actions until they first deal with the hangups which are preventing change. Often the intrapsychic (inner) causes of the breakdown in interpersonal relations must be dealt with first.

After Phil's mother died, when he was a boy of ten, he lived alone with his father for many years. After a while, the father began drinking heavily and at times would abuse him, occasionally even in sexual ways. The house was unkempt and dirty and Phil could never bring friends home. For several years, there was a steady stream of women who spent the night with his father. At an early age, Phil was overloaded with responsibility and became a loner. In one of our sessions, as he was sharing his story, he allowed himself to plug into his emotions. With moist eyes and a trembling voice he said, *"I guess I learned to cope with all this by just never allowing myself to feel anything. I didn't dare let myself feel good in the occasional happy times because I knew they couldn't last. And I didn't dare allow myself to cry or feel down because I just had to keep going. I guess the truth of the matter is that I've been afraid to let myself feel. And now I don't know how."*

Phil had an unusual request—he wanted Janet to be with him when we went through the prayer time for the healing of those painful memories. She was very understanding and held him, yes, like his much-needed mother, while we all wept and prayed together. Phil needed to courageously face many unpleasant and painful memories. As they came to mind he had to do a lot of forgiving of his father and receive a lot of forgiveness from God for his resentments.

When he became free from these chains of the past, he

and Janet were both able to begin making the proper behavioral changes which had been recommended to them. This was by no means easy; it was hard work and required much encouragement and counseling, *but at least it was now possible, whereas before it was not.* Why? Because the kind of love required for those changes was not possible until first some "childish things" were put away—*katargeod*—rendered inoperative and powerless to interfere with his present adult efforts. The healing of his memories freed him so that he could now allow himself to feel. This was an absolutely necessary first step in learning how to express his feelings for Janet. And this kind of inner healing was perfectly consistent with the biblical principle we have stated.

Accept Christ as a Present Helper

Jesus Christ is our eternal contemporary, the Lord of time and our healer; and His Holy Spirit is our present and available helper. The most distinctive part of the healing of memories is the time of prayer. Through the use of imagination, we try to recreate the painful memory and then actually visualize it as it once took place. We pray as if we were actually talking to God on the spot and ask Him to do for us what we would have asked, had we prayed then and there. We ask Him to heal the little child or teenager who underwent those experiences— things which really did fixate the child at that place, which made him get stuck at that stage of growth. How can this be possible when the events may have happened many years ago in time? How can our prayers today possibly affect that inner child or youngster of the long-ago past?

The Scriptures tell us that Christ is the Lord of time—

past, present, and future. In a very real sense He is our eternal contemporary, "the same yesterday, today, and forever" (Hebrews 13:8). When John the Baptist introduced Jesus to the people, he said, "Here is the One I was speaking about when I said that although He would come after me He would always be in front of me; for He existed before I was born!" (John 1:15, PH) In another passage there is a wonderful mix-up of tenses. When the Jews taunted our Lord, "You are not yet fifty years old, and have You seen Abraham?" He answered them with, "Truly, truly, I say to you, before Abraham was, I am" (John 8:57-58, RSV).

If Christ could make these statements during His incarnate earthly existence, how much more can we now make them of the risen, ascended, and glorified Christ! He transcends all time and space, which are, after all, finite concepts of the limitations on our human lives. As Jesus demonstrated on numerous occasions following His resurrection, He was not limited by either time or space, but could appear anywhere and anytime. In a sense, it all is present tense with Him. Because we are bound by time and space, we say Christ "walks back into time" in order to minister to some hurting person. Because of our finite limitations, we do not understand *how* He does this, but we can certainly *visualize Him doing it.* Indeed, on the basis of Scripture, we have every right to picture Him as *here and now.*

But is all this mere autosuggestion? A sort of self-hypnosis where we "psych" ourselves out by the use of mental pictures and strong imagination? No. The promises regarding the work of the Holy Spirit's participating presence and power assure us He really is here. It is the Holy Spirit who makes the trancendent Christ intimately immanent. The Spirit assures us He is truly alongside us, "taking hold along with us over on the other side." Later we shall look at some of the pictures of Jesus which are helpful in healing of the memories. While they are pictures based on biblical symbols, the *form* of the mental images by which we visualize His presence is the product of our imaginations. But the *fact* of His presence pictured by these images is guaranteed by the promises of Scripture.

There is a lovely hymn by Henry Twells which we often sang prior to the monthly evening healing services in our church. It beautifully expresses the healing power of Christ who is always with us in the present tense (*The Book of Hymns*, United Methodist Publishing House, p. 501).

> At even, ere the sun was set,
> The sick, O Lord, around Thee lay;
> O in what divers pains they met!
> O with what joy they went away!
>
> Once more 'tis eventide, and we,
> Oppressed with various ills, draw near;
> What if Thy form we cannot see?
> We know and feel that Thou art here.
>
> O Saviour Christ, our woes dispel,
> For some are sick, and some are sad,
> And some have never loved Thee well,
> And some have lost the love they had.
>
> And none, O Lord, have perfect rest,
> For none are wholly free from sin;
> And they who fain would serve Thee best
> Are conscious most of wrong within.

O Saviour Christ, Thou too art man,
Thou hast been troubled, tempted, tried;
Thy kind but searching glance can scan
The very wounds that shame would hide.

Thy touch has still its ancient power,
No word from Thee can fruitless fall;
Hear, in this solemn evening hour,
And in Thy mercy heal us all.

Pray Specifically

We need to be specific in our confessions and prayers. One of the great emphases of Scripture is the need for ruthless moral honesty in facing our sins, failures, and needs. In the very first story of human disobedience in the Garden, we see the human tendency to cover up when any kind of emotional pain is involved. When the Lord God came down for His usual time of fellowship with Adam and Eve, they hid from His presence among the trees of the Garden. When God called out to Adam asking where he was, he answered, "I was afraid because I was naked; so I hid myself" (Genesis 3:8-10). Ever since then, we humans have been afraid to be open and uncovered, not only with God but also with others *and ourselves.* It is this fear gone to extremes in our fallen, distorted personalities that we see in repressed memories which cause us pain. We cover and hide them rather than face them. This covertness permeates our personalities in every realm. It is the leading cause of our fear and guilt and, more than anything else, disrupts our relationships.

The biblical prescription for this endemic human disease is honesty, openness, repentance, and confession. Jesus called the Holy Spirit "The Spirit of Truth" (John

14—16). The Apostle John used the word *truth* twenty-two times in his Gospel and nine times in his First Epistle. In 1 John, we see a direct correlation between truth, confession, and our relationship to God, others, and ourselves. Let me explain.

Centuries before the branch of learning we call psychology ever began, John described what we now know as our defense mechanisms. These are simply the various ways we humans keep from seeing the truth, and protect ourselves from fear and anxiety. They don't change the reality or truth of the situation; they only change the way we look at it. We actually protect ourselves by deceiving ourselves, so that we won't have to change. Let's look at the Apostle John's words:

> And this is the message we have heard from Him and announce to you, that God is light, and in Him there is no darkness at all. If we say that we have fellowship with Him and yet walk in darkness, we lie and do not practice the truth; but if we walk in the light as He Himself is in the light, we have fellowship with one another, and the blood of Jesus His Son cleanses us from all sin.
>
> If we say that we have no sin, we are deceiving ourselves, and the truth is not in us. If we confess our sins, He is faithful and righteous to forgive us our sins and to cleanse us from all unrighteousness. If we say that we have not sinned, we make Him a liar, and His word is not in us (1 John 1:5-10).

Now let us see how both John and the psychologists describe the three main defense mechanisms. These are given in the order of their seriousness.

• Denial. This is the simplest and most direct of them all. We just plain deny something; we lie about it. We refuse to acknowledge it; we don't want to look at it or discuss it. John comments on this: "If we say that we have fellowship with Him and yet walk in darkness, we lie and do not practice the truth" (v. 6).

• Rationalization. This means of defense is more complicated and, therefore, more serious. It is not as outright as lying, but is more sophisticated. Here we try to give reasons which justify our behavior. Someone has said there are two reasons for everything we do: a *good* reason and the *real* reason! We not only deceive someone else, but now we deceive ourselves; it is a deeper deception than denial or lying because we are often unaware of it. John deals with this: "If we refuse to admit that we are sinners, then we live in a world of illusion and truth becomes a stranger to us" (v. 8, PH).

• Projection. This is the worst of them all because here we take deception one step further and blame others for our problems. In fact, we project our failures onto someone or something else and say *they have the problem*. John describes this so accurately: "We make Him (God) a liar and His Word is not in us" (v. 10). Whereas we began by telling the lie ourselves, we end up by saying God is telling the lie. "I'm not the liar; *He is!*"

Now I realize this passage of Scripture is set in the context of moral and spiritual matters. But it has a definite bearing on our subject, for its principles also extend to the emotional/spiritual areas of life. One of the reasons that unhealed memories can cause such disruption in our lives is that they usually contain many negative emotions, such as fear, hurt, anger, guilt, shame, and anxiety. Again and again these feelings arise and we wonder where they are coming from. We feel confused because we are unable to pinpoint the cause of the feelings. This makes us feel guilty, because "Christians are not supposed to have such feelings." So we not only have the problem, but we double back on ourselves with added guilt for ever having the problem. The difficulty lies in the fact that *we are unable to pray specifically about it.* It's like trying to fight a fog. What we desperately need is to be able to discover the place of specific need—to find out what the real problem is so we can then deal with it. The principle involved here is a very important one: *We cannot confess to God what we do not acknowledge to ourselves.* And so we make our generalized confessions, give and receive generalized forgiveness, and end up with a hazy, foggy, generalized relationship with God.

We do not intend it to be this way; but because *a lot of specifics are protected by our defense mechanisms and hidden in our buried memories, we cannot find emotional and spiritual relief from their onslaughts.* We need to uncover the situations, experiences, and attitudes which are causing the negative emotions and allow the Holy Spirit to deal with them specifically. And this is exactly what happens so often during the healing of memories prayer time. Instead of the general prayers, "O Lord, please help me to have better feelings toward my parents, or help me to forgive my brother, or sister," now the specific hurt is mentioned in detail. "O Lord, I was so hurt that day Daddy threw my toy across the room and broke it because I had accidentally spilled water on his book, and then he made fun of me when I cried. I was so angry, I really hated him for that. I was really glad when he had the accident that afternoon." Or, "Father, I have never really forgiven my teacher, Mrs. Slade, for humiliating me that day in front of the whole class, and accusing me of something another kid had done. And I've wanted to get even with Johnny for lying about it. I forgive them for what they did to me; and I need You to forgive me, Lord, for these years of resentment toward them." And on and on it goes. *Specific memories* which have finally been allowed to surface, resulting in *specific confessions of specific feelings; specific forgiveness* given and received, resulting in deep inner healing and cleansing. This principle of specificity is central to the healing of memories and is in perfect accord with the biblical truths regarding repentance, confession, and healing.

Time and again I have seen the turning point in a person's healing come when his memories plugged in to some important details he had pushed out of his mind. Joyce was a competent social worker in her late twenties. Engaged to be married, she had moved to our part of the country to be near her fiancé. Within six months he broke the engagement. She was crushed and sought help, for the shock of the rejection forced her to realize that this was a pattern in all of her relationships with men. Although Joyce had been a Christian for several years, she had a lot of trouble with mood swings, depression, and a general sense of hostility toward men. She commuted to work in a car pool and the other women didn't like when it was her turn to drive. They told her she scared them because she drove "angrily." Two of her companions were married. Joyce noticed that the happier their marriages were, the angrier she got; she was jealous of their good relationships. On the job her coworkers watched her short fuse and volatile temper. Besides her broken engagement, it was what one of them had said to her that jolted her into realizing she needed counseling. "Joyce, you certainly are an even-tempered person— you're always mad."

In counseling, Joyce told of a home in which there was an unbelievable amount of drinking, conflict, and fighting. Caring Christians had helped her find a church family and a new life in Christ. But the lack of fatherly affection and love left its toll, and she constantly sought to fill the empty hole in her heart through a series of boyfriends. It was always the same pattern—desperately reaching out for affection, she would become too physically involved with her steadies. Although her Christian moral standards prevented her from going "all the way," she would become very intimate with them. This would result in a loss of self-respect and usually end up in a breakup. Joyce was very discouraged and angry at her own compulsions. She was sure this was God's way of punishing her and that He would never allow her to have a lasting relationship and a husband.

We went through a long list of hurts and hates, humiliations and guilts during a lengthy prayer time. A whole river of emotion was released, and after considerable struggle she found grace to forgive and be washed of her bitterness. Then, when I thought we were about finished, the Spirit pulled back the veil of remembrance and sharpened her memory. Specific details of a sordid night spent with a man became crystal clear. She cried out in agonizing prayer as she relived the terrible feelings she experienced. "O Jesus, I feel so terrible. I have let myself down, and failed You in my witness. I have lost all respect for myself; I have no faith in myself to carry out my convictions. I give up on myself—and I feel that You have given up on me too."

She then realized that that night had been a turning point of self-hate and despair. Ever since then she had felt God was punishing her; she had been punishing herself by her self-destructive sexual behavior. In prayer, she now allowed a merciful and loving God to minister to her as she relived that awful night. He forgave her and gave her back her sense of virtue and self-worth as a woman. It was a blessed time of cleansing and restoration. What a joy it was two years later to be the officiating minister at her marriage to a deeply dedicated young man. The most beautiful part of the ceremony was when they both shared how God had taken the broken pieces of their lives and reconstructed them, now giving them the gift of a new beginning. We've talked about transformation several times since. She always reminds me that the healing change began when she could confess to God a lot of specifics which, prior to then, she had prayed about only in generalities.

Minister to One Another

The Body-Life principle means that Christians minister to one another for healing. James enunciated this truth in his epistle: "And the prayer offered in faith will restore the one who is sick, and the Lord will raise him up, and if he has committed sins, they will be forgiven him. Therefore, confess your sins to one another and pray for one another, so that you may be healed" (James 5:15-16).

Our Lord Himself, in His great teachings on prayer, gave us the promise of corporate prayer. "I say to you, that if two of you agree on earth about anything that they may ask, it shall be done for them by My Father who is in heaven. For where two or three have gathered together in My name, there I am in their midst" (Matthew 18:19-20).

The kind of prayer which takes place during the healing of memories fits perfectly with the commands to "confess to one another," and to "agree" about the subject before they ask for an answer. The Scriptures recognize that some petitions require a corporate, open, and sharing kind of prayer before they will be answered. Once again both the "confession" and the "agreeing" assume the specificity which God honors. I think it is significant that the verse prior to the "agreeing" promise tells us, "Whatever you shall bind on earth shall have been bound in heaven; and whatever you loose on earth shall have been loosed in heaven." And the verses which follow contain some of the most important teachings on the subject of forgiving and being forgiven that we find anywhere in the New Testament. Surely all this fits most perfectly in the context of praying for the healing of memories. It seems in God's plan there are certain kinds of healings—physical, emotional, and spiritual—which can come about only through the ministry of other members of the Body of Christ.

Confession and Restoration

I would be remiss if I did not close this chapter by pointing out that this particular biblical principle is now being fully confirmed by the latest findings in medicine and psychology. In the *Lexington Herald-Leader*, Lexington, Kentucky, September 23, 1984, an article appeared from the *New York Times* News Service. It was entitled, "Confession May Be Good for Body," and it went on to say, "Confession, whatever it may do for the soul, appears to be good for the body. New studies show persuasively that people who are able to confide in others about their troubled feelings or some traumatic event, rather than bear the turmoil in silence, are less vulnerable to disease." It then reported on several different experiments which confirm the "long-term health benefits" of sharing our most painful secrets with others.

Dr. James Pennebaker's research shows that "the act of confiding in someone else protects the body against damaging internal stresses that are the penalty for carrying around an onerous emotional burden such as unspoken remorse." Similar research conducted at Harvard University shows that those who do not share have "less effective immune systems." Dr. Pennebaker, of Johns Hopkins School of Medicine, publishing his findings in *The Journal of Abnormal Psychology*, confirms these discoveries.

How interesting that modern science is just now catching up with the plain teachings of Scripture. David declared these truths thousands of years ago.

How blessed is he whose transgression is forgiven,
Whose sin is covered!
How blessed is the man to whom
the Lord does not impute iniquity,
And in whose spirit there is no deceit!
When I kept silent about my sin, my body
wasted away through my groaning all day long.
For day and night Thy hand was heavy upon me;
My vitality was drained away
as with the fever-heat of summer.
I acknowledged my sin to Thee,
And my iniquity I did not hide;
I said, "I will confess my transgressions to the Lord."
And Thou didst forgive the guilt of my sin.
Therefore, let everyone who is godly pray to Thee
in a time when Thou mayest be found. . . .
Thou art my hiding place:
Thou dost preserve me from trouble:
Thou dost surround me with songs of deliverance.
(Psalm 32:1-7)

Is there an example in the Bible where the principles we have described were actually used to heal someone's painful memories? Yes, in the way Jesus handled Peter's denial and restoration. There are only two places in the New Testament where the word for a "charcoal fire" is used. In John 18:18 we are told that Peter stood with the servants and officers in the courtyard warming himself before a "charcoal fire." It was there he denied Jesus three times. Later, on the beach that post-Resurrection morning, when Jesus prepared breakfast for the disciples, He deliberately set the stage for Peter (John 21:9). Once again there was the "charcoal fire." Jesus, master Physician and Psychiatrist, forced Peter to stand near a charcoal fire. Oh, how his memories and his shame must have burned within him. Three times he had denied his Lord and three times he was asked to affirm his love for Him—standing before those hot red coals. Jesus used a fire of coals, somewhat like a "coal off the altar of fire" used by the Lord in Isaiah 6, to cauterize and heal Peter's pain and shame. As he faced pain in all of its specifics, his memories were healed, and he was restored and recommissioned for service.

6
INDICATIONS FOR
THE HEALING
OF MEMORIES

WHAT ARE SOME of the symptoms which point to the possible need for the healing of memories? I say *possible*, because all along I have been stressing that the healing of memories is one, and only one, form of inner healing. I would reemphasize that here. The kinds of emotional/ spiritual dysfunctions which will be described do not automatically mean memory healing is the only spiritual therapy that should be considered.

When painful memories have not been faced, healed, and integrated into life, they often break through defenses and interfere with normal living.

One of the evidences of this is recurring mental pictures, scenes, or dreams which bring disturbance and disruption to the emotional and spiritual life.

During the counseling process, I always ask a question something like this: "Do you have certain pictures in your mind which keep coming back? Which won't seem to let you alone, but keep repeating themselves over and over again? Or perhaps which keep recurring in your dreams? Mental images (memories) which are so strong they actually interfere with your present life?" If the answer is affirmative, I request that the person tell me about them.

While the particulars may be drastically different, the facts are the same. There are certain mental pictures which keep coming back like TV video replays. Sometimes they are like the replays in slow motion, which means that *the emotions which go along with the memories are very intense.* It is like the super-slow motion of the game, when you actually *see and feel* the determination or the pain on the player's face! Often these recurring playbacks are strongest just before dropping off to sleep, or while waking during the night, or just before awakening in the morning. Sometimes they are in dreams (nightmares) in which the victims discover themselves screaming, struggling, or in a cold sweat. These can be so intense as to affect their ability to cope with life the following day.

The characters and the plots of the recurring scenes are as varied as the lives of those involved. However, I have noticed the contents and the pain seem to have certain of the following common denominators.

Hurts

In one sense, anything which causes physical pain or mental and emotional anguish could be called a hurt. I will confine this discussion to some of the more common experiences of life which cause emotional suffering by striking a blow to a person's selfhood. Our present word *hurt* comes from the older Middle English words *hurten, hirten,* "to strike or harm," which in turn come from the Old French *hurter* (*American Heritage Dictionary of the English Language*). Whatever strikes or harms our ego causes us hurt. This can happen to us at any level of life, from the prenatal stage, infancy, childhood, the teens, through young adulthood, and on to old age. At the very heart of many of our hurts is *a sense of rejection.* The more important or significant the rejecting person is to us, the greater is our feeling of being rejected by him.

The most painful kinds of rejection occur during the earliest years of life—preschool and the early grades—because there is no way of explaining the reason for an action which infants or children interpret as rejection. Children cannot understand why they are being treated that way, and they don't know how to cope with it. There may be very logical reasons for what is taking place, but there is no way of communicating them or of their being properly understood. For example, many of the most deeply felt rejections result from accidents, illnesses, unavoidable delays, or even deaths. Parents, family members, relatives, teachers, pastors, or friends are forced by the circumstances to give something or someone else prime time and priority attention. This is experienced as a rejection and can leave a painful scar on the memories.

Jeff, a very earnest Christian young man, came seeking help for his low self-esteem, depression, and spiritual defeats. He had an almost constant fear of being abandoned by family, friends, and even by God. Strange feelings of lonely uneasiness which stirred up hazy memories would come back to him again and again. In various ways this uneasiness was the theme of many situations which haunted his dreams. But it was all so foggy that he was hard put to describe it very clearly. Of one thing he was

sure—*rejection was in the center of it all.* We had no difficulty in observing Jeff's reactions. In such situations, the
core of hurt is so painful that the person develops the
additional problem of becoming terribly afraid of being
hurt (in Jeff's case, rejected) in the same way again. This
becomes a vicious circle—like a dog chasing its own tail
and occasionally biting it! So the fear of additional rejection and further hurt grows and grows until it affects the
person's perception of life. The fear becomes an expectation and this finally becomes the *hurtful filter* through
which he screens the most ordinary experiences of life.
All this causes him to *feel* a great deal more pain than he
is actually experiencing in his present circumstances.

With Jeff, it was easy to trace this painful progression;
he was now living in a kind of carefully insulated space
capsule which protected him from more of the anticipated
wounds. So we began where he was and slowly moved
backward in time, using various methods we will describe
in a later chapter. We, of course, also surrounded our
sessions with much prayer, constantly asking for the understanding and discernment which only the Holy Spirit
can give. One of my earliest mentors described this process by an unforgettable picture which has been of great
help in my counseling. He advised me, "Sometimes you
just have to keep on rowing and praying, praying and
rowing, until the Spirit shows you the right place to
land!"

One day the Spirit showed Jeff and me the proper
memory dock, and after landing, He guided us to explore
a labyrinth of hidden caves filled with feelings of abandonment and rejection. It had all begun at the birth of a
baby sister, when Jeff was four years old. His mother had
undergone a difficult pregnancy and an extremely painful
delivery. To make matters worse, his sister had been born

with a correctable birth defect which required a lot of attention and considerable expense. Up to this point, Jeff had been the center of the family care and affection. Now there was a drastic shift. Under the most normal circumstances, this "redistribution of love" is difficult enough. In Jeff's case, it was traumatic. In many families, the older child makes the adjustment by becoming "Mama's Little Helper" and is thus made an important part of the enlarged system. But the nature of the newborn's problems excluded Jeff from even this role. Quite unintentionally, Jeff was left out and felt extremely hurt by what he perceived as deliberate rejection. There were extended periods when the sister required treatment by specialists in a distant town, and Jeff was left with an unmarried aunt who did not comprehend the change in Jeff's behavior. Instead of giving him much-needed extra understanding and love, she only added extra discipline and punishment. Jeff's hurt and rejection were compounded by confused feelings of fear, anger, and guilt. He was sure that it was something he had done which had caused the whole situation—his mother's morning sickness, the difficult delivery, and the birth defect. Like every child, he had ambivalent feelings of love and anger toward his mother and baby sister—*was God punishing him for those wrong thoughts and feelings?* He pushed those unacceptable feelings out of his mind, but life seemed to become increasingly unfair and painful. To a grown-up this may sound ridiculous, but on a four-year-old level, it has a consistent sense of logic and reason.

As we shared and prayed together, Jeff began to recall in graphic detail the vicious circle of hurt, fear of more hurt, and the distorted perceptions which presumed additional rejection and hurt. As a series of memories emerged, he was astounded at the deep feelings of rage and bitterness toward his sister and aunt which erupted along with them. During the prayer time I was reminded of the story in John 5. . . . you remember, the people claimed God sent an angel to trouble the waters of the pool which then became healing waters. In a similar way, God stirred up Jeff's mind for emotional and spiritual hydrotherapy. The only way healing became possible was for him to step right down into this pool of troubled memories, painful as this was. It took several trips (dips) into the pool to receive adequate wholeness. Each time, we asked Jesus to give Jeff the understanding, love, affection, and forgiveness he needed at a particular stage of his childhood. Finally, the propulsive and compulsive intensity of his recurring memories and dreams was dissolved, and Jeff was able to learn mature and Christian ways of relating to others. Of course, he had to work hard at reprogramming his outlook and learning new relationships. However, *because of the healing of his memories he was now free to do so.* Prior to this, in spite of much effort and spiritual discipline, he had not been able to do so.

Humiliations

Another common theme of these recurring painful flashbacks is embarrassment, shame, and humiliation. A party game or TV program based on "My Most Embarrassing Moment" may be very entertaining. Those are the incidents we have worked through and can even laugh at. But memories involving times when we were deeply humiliated produce the most painful emotions we experience, and are some of the chief causes of low self-esteem and depression. Stanley, a minister in his forties, shared this story with a small group at a Yokefellow retreat one weekend. It was his first day at school and he was very proud of the fact that he could write his name. So when the teacher asked who could write his name, he was the first pupil to volunteer. He took out a piece of paper and spelled it out in big block letters—STANLEY.

"She said, "You've spelled it wrong. It's spelled STANDLEY."

He replied timidly, "No, Ma'am, there's no D in my name."

"Write it again," she said sternly, "and spell it right this time."

Stanley wrote it again, without the D. She scooped up the paper, held it before the whole class, turning so all could see, "Look, boys and girls. Here's a boy who's so stupid he doesn't even know how to spell his own name. Now Stanley, write your name again and put the D in it this time, do you hear?"

So he did as he was ordered. His spirit was crushed and he felt shattered inside when some of the children around him tittered with laughter at his deep crimson blush.

Stanley commented on the incident to his share group, "That scene seems stamped on my mind forever. I cringe and hurt inside every time I think of how the class laughed when she told them how stupid I was. And worst of all, for some weird reason, I accepted her evaluation. The crazy thing is that I still feel stupid. I know it doesn't make any sense—my wife, my accomplishments, my people—all tell me I'm not stupid. But there's an inner voice that says I am." He added, "Not long ago I was talking to one of my members who has a Ph.D. He told me he had been helped greatly by our conversation and paid me a genuine, high compliment. And you know what? Something inside me said immediately, "Well, he may have a Ph.D., but he must be pretty dumb not to see how stupid and inadequate I really am!"

It's amazing how insensitive parents, teachers, and other authority figures can be to the devastating effects of public put-downs on children. With the best of intentions, these adults often use the put-down as a form of discipline or a way of changing behavior. Because it brings rapid results, they think it is legitimate. They fail to realize the deep damage to the fragile self-esteem of tenderhearted youngsters, because of agonizing memories which are literally branded on their minds.

Scripture has much to teach us at this point. God's Spirit usually came to people and dealt with their shameful failures privately. How careful Jesus was to do this— He confronted people with their sins and mistakes when they were alone with Him. Indeed, He went out of His way to defend and build them up before others, waiting for the opportune private moment to take up the negatives. In His advice, in Matthew 18:15-17, Jesus was careful to lay down principles for dealing with all such situations. First we speak to people privately and try to correct situations. Only when that doesn't succeed do we gradually add others (witnesses) until finally there is the public admonition. When Paul gave the updated version of the fifth commandment (parent-child relationships) in Ephesians 6:1-4, he exhorted fathers not to do anything which would deliberately goad their children to resentment.

However, not all the recurring memories of humiliation are necessarily public. Some of them involve private situations when cruel and thoughtless remarks are etched deeply on the walls of the imagination.

One beautiful woman, who battled low self-esteem for many years, shared with great pain the mental picture which arose almost every time she put on her makeup. She had been brought up in a very strict home where her father considered any form of makeup sinful. One morning, in her preteens, she used some face powder to cover the skin blemishes which often occur at that age. Here are her very own words as she recalled this hurtful humiliation, "My Dad laughed at me and sarcastically commented that I looked like a white-faced heifer." And then she added with significant emotion, *"And not once while I was growing up did he ever tell me that I looked nice."*

Thinking back, we were able to understand why her dad had done this. He was afraid that her attractiveness would "get her into trouble with the boys." Downgrading her appearance was his mistaken way of protecting her virtue. Sad to say, this is a mistake many parents make, when they have handsome sons or beautiful daughters. That they mean no harm does not lessen the emotional wreckage. All too often their attempts to control by guilt, shame, and humiliation become the seedbed of painful memories which someday will need healing.

Sometimes memories of humiliation are not connected with specific incidents, but are part of the overall atmosphere of the growing years. We find this especially in connection with an alcoholic parent. The family becomes a part of the system which has to cover for mother's or dad's drinking problem. So the child or teenager becomes adept at making excuses for not being able to invite friends in. A way of life which includes half-truths and plausible reasons fills the youngster with shame and deceit. Feelings of being different from others and always cheated out of fun times poisons their memories with the pain of humiliation.

Horrors

I am using this strong word to cover the gamut of fears and terrors which can lie embedded in the lower layers of the mind and one day rise to fill us with all kinds of anxieties. It would require an encyclopedia to cover all the different ways the roots of fear become embedded in our memories. It is said there are 365 "Fear nots" in the Bible—one for each day of the year. This is because God knows what it's like to live in this fear-filled world; He understands that these deep-seated fears are some of our greatest obstacles to faith.

Some of the most common and disabling fears shared with me for memory healing include the following:

> fear of the dark,
> fear of being abandoned or left alone,
> fear of failure, not accomplishing anything worthwhile,
> fear of losing one's mind or control of one's emotions,
> fear of sex, sexual thoughts, and desires,
> fear of people and trusting others,
> fear of cancer and other serious illnesses,
> fear of God and the final judgment,
> fear of committing the "unpardonable sin,"
> fear of the future,
> fear of death of others close to us, or our own.

Among Christians, many of these fears are greatly intensified by a sense of guilt for having the fear in the first place. Good Christians are not supposed to be anxious or afraid—after all, Jesus is always with them and so there is nothing to be afraid of. Besides, the Bible says, "Perfect love casts out fear" (1 John 4:18). And so they become all the more afraid and are trapped in a vicious cycle of being afraid to admit they are afraid!

The fact is, many of these fears are rooted in frightening experiences, unhealthy teachings, and poor relationships somewhere in the past, especially during the early years of childhood. They have been pushed to the bottom level of the mind so often that the person may have only the haziest memories of them. Often there are not specific remembrances and the individual is plagued with general, global feelings of anxiety which attach themselves to first one thing and then another.

It was like this with Jack and Jill, brother and sister in a very emotionally disturbed family. The father was a religious tyrant and the mother a religious doormat. He ruled "by the Book," meaning his own inflexible (and usually wrong) interpretations of the Bible, backed up by an unpredictable temper which sometimes bordered on violence. The mother survived and tried to maintain peace and hold the family together by "sweet submission." The result was an atmosphere where everyone walked on emotional eggshells before the father. And before the Heavenly Father as well, because of the faulty earthly model and his dogmatic half-truths. It was the kind of religious home which Christian counselors confront so often. We are always amazed at the amount of emotional and spiritual wreckage wrought in the name of twisted Scripture—especially the Ephesians 5:21—6:4 passage which describes marriage and family relationships.

The memories which caused Jack's fears were so deeply submerged that when they came out, they were mixed into a great variety of biblical and theological questions. I could expect a regular phone call from Jack every few weeks. They always went something like this, "I was reading in the Bible recently and came across a passage where it says thus and so, and this has bothered me a lot. I'm afraid that I . . . " or "I don't understand how . . . ." This would be the preface introducing an area of great anxiety which was troubling Jack's spiritual life. It was not until Jack could recall and face the painful and horrifying climate of his developmental years that he was able to be healed of its memories and find wholesomeness in both his emotions and his beliefs.

Jill's fears came out in a quite different way—all kinds of illnesses, some very real and some imaginary. Jill's mother had paid an awful price for her failure to confront the true situation and express her real feelings. When she could stand it no longer, she took to bed. This brought her some much-needed attention, even tenderness, from her husband. He, in turn, used it as another means of controlling the children—"Be quiet now; don't upset your mother and make her sicker than you already have."

Jill had learned well from her mother, and her life also had an unpredictable atmosphere; different, but equally fearful. Crippling pains, a forty-eight hour virus, or even some kind of heart condition could strike at any time. And so Jill, like the woman mentioned in Mark 5:26, "endured much at the hands of many physicians, and . . . spent all that she had and was not helped at all." It seemed as if Jill wore a coat of fear and kept looking for an illness to hang it on. Healing of some ancient memories, and then lots of practice at learning other ways of coping with responsibility, have enabled Jill to lead a reasonably stable life.

Hates

We come to an area which is at the very heart of our subject—resentment, bitterness, and hate. In a later chapter we shall show how to deal with our hates, through the prayers for forgiving and being forgiven. At this point, we are considering hate as one of the major ingredients in those recurring mental replays which are a sign we may need a healing of some painful memories. For everything we have described in this chapter usually brings with it strong resentments. Sometimes we are quite conscious of these and struggle against them in prayer, but seemingly to no avail. Sometimes we are simply aware that general feelings of rage are within us, but we are unable to pinpoint the causes. They seem to be submerged just below the level of our conscious recall. This is often the cause of depression among Christians, this frozen and buried resentment. At other times, the stress from this repressed hate expresses itself through the body language of sickness. There are many illnesses which may have their roots in unhealed resentments. There is the classic story of the youngster who overheard his dad telling someone his mother had colitis. He sighed and asked his father, "Who has she been colliding with now?"

You remember when Jesus was riding into Jerusalem, in that event we call the Triumphal Entry, that the religious authorities told Him to make the people stop shouting their Hosannas and expressing their emotions. Jesus replied that if He didn't allow the people to express themselves, "the very stones would cry out" (Luke 19:40). There is a living parable in this story. When Christians fail to express their true feelings, their bodies cry out through the voices of pain and illness. This is especially true of resentments buried so deep they are not even allowed to enter into conscious memories. These occasionally burst through into the mind and then the slow-motion video replays occur. Scenes and pictures arise and rage takes over. Christians are particularly confused when they then "take it out" on someone nearby—a spouse or a child they dearly love. This, in turn, fills them with remorse, guilt, and spiritual defeat. They are further bewildered because they can't figure out where it all comes from. Most likely they unwittingly drilled into some ancient and untapped river of resentment which, like a sudden oil strike, "blew" up. When this keeps happening and doesn't seem to be helped by discipline, prayer, and deeper experiences in the Spirit, we should look for the causes in the pressure and pain of unhealed memories.

Perhaps the most puzzling and shocking experience of all is when devout Christians find themselves overrun by feelings of anger against God Himself. This is terribly hard to admit. I have spent many sessions gently leading counselees to the place where they finally realized their resentment against God. The shock has been so great that some have momentarily passed out in my office, or have became nauseated to the point of vomiting. For they love God and want to serve and please Him and are devastated when they discover this submerged anger against Him. After the initial trauma passes, they are able to take their bitter feelings into His very presence and let Him wash them away in His love. Later, as we look back, we see this very act of remembering and feeling was the necessary breakthrough and the beginning of their healing.

It was this way with one man who shared with me some of the worst stories of child abuse I have ever heard. It was hard to imagine the ingenious ways his mother used to hurt him, exquisite acts of physical torture and verbal decimation. Being a good Christian, he had never really faced his true feelings about all this. Instead, he kept assuring me how much he loved his mother. Little by little, the painful details came out and he became aware of a violent rage against her. But underneath this was an even deeper layer of anger. One day, right in the middle of our prayers for healing these horrible memories, he cried out in anguish, *"And God, where in the hell were You when all this was going on?"* A flood of violent emotion gripped him. In his fear he shook like a leaf. But it wasn't long before he experienced a flood of God's love washing over him like ocean waves. Years of reprogramming and therapy have been necessary for his wholeness, but there is no doubt that this moment was the beginning of a great healing in his life.

In a truly remarkable book, *May I Hate God?* by Pierre Wolff (Paulist Press), the author shows how our anger and resentment, which we think will only separate us from God, can also become the doorway to greater intimacy with Him. It is a small book and I recommend it to those who are afraid to face this painful area of their spiritual lives. I have found it very useful in preparing people for the healing of memories prayer time.

And so we have taken an entire chapter to consider the primary symptom which indicates the need for memory healing—that is, recurring mental pictures and memories which are so intense they interfere with present behavior.

We are now going to spend the next two chapters on a second symptom—distorted and destructive concepts of God.

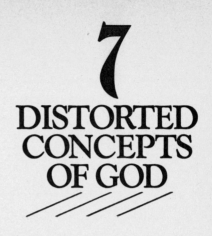

DISTORTED CONCEPTS OF GOD

INSIDE EVERY ONE OF US is a mental picture of God. We often speak of this as our concept of God and talk about it as if it were something completely in our minds. We forget that, along with what we have been taught about God, experiences, memories, and feelings play a large part in forming this picture. *The most determinative factor is our "feltness" of who God is and what He is really like.* It is surprising the number of genuine Christians who are caught in an inner conflict between what they *think* about God and what they *feel* about God (and how He feels toward them). Their head *theology* is excellent but their gut-level *knee-ology* (what they feel when they pray) is terrible. This is the source of many emotional hangups in Christians and one of the strongest indicators for a healing of memories. Years of experience have taught me that regardless of how much correct doctrine Christians may know, *until they have a picture and a felt sense that God is truly good and gracious, there can be no lasting spiritual victory in their lives.*

The Good News and the Bad News

How is it that the Gospel which we proclaim as Good News so often becomes bad news that affects our feelings?

To understand this, let's borrow a concept from foreign missions—cross-cultural evangelism. In a short time, a missionary becomes aware of the fact that what the people hear him say can be very different from what he has actually said. He proclaims (encodes) something, but the listener hears (decodes) something else. While working in India, I soon learned to be very careful about preaching on the text "You must be born again" (John 3:7). The Hindu decodes those words through his belief system of reincarnation and a cycle of rebirths. So he hears it as, "You must be born again and again and again," going through many reincarnations until one finds salvation (release) from the cycle.

Or, let's bring it closer to home—literally. I say the word *home.* To some the word means "heaven," and their mental images and feelings correspond to that. To others it means "hell," and they see and feel correspondingly. Our concepts are composite mental pictures made up of many different pieces which come to us from various sources. Chief among those which contribute to our concept of God are life experiences, interpersonal relationships, and teachings we have been given. Certainly, what we have been *taught* is extremely important. But what we have *caught* is equally so. In fact, *our feelings about God can drastically affect our ideas of God.* This is because those feelings are part of the dynamics which determine the way we perceive the teachings given to us. *This crucial fact is overlooked by so many pastors and Christian workers.* They assume if the doctrines and ideas they preach and teach are biblically correct, they will automatically clear up a person's concepts of God and enable him to believe in God and trust Him. They imagine that the Holy Spirit, as it were, somehow drills a hole in the top of the hearer's head and pours the pure truth into him.

With many people, nothing could be further from the truth. For although the Holy Spirit is the One who reveals the truth, what the listener hears and pictures and feels still has to be filtered through him. The Holy Spirit Himself does not bypass the personality equipment by which a person perceives things. *And when those perceiving receptors have been severely damaged, the biblical truths get distorted.*

In this sense the facetious remark—"Man creates God in his own image"—contains an element of truth. Even for the most healthy and normal Christians, clarifying their concepts of God is a lifelong task and a central part of reaching maturity in Christ. This is one of the main reasons why the Incarnation was so necessary. The Word had to become *flesh.* God had gone as far as He could in revealing Himself through *words.* For at their very best— as in the greatest prophets of the Old Testament—words are subject to the distortions of sinful and damaged hearers. Only when the Word became a human life was it possible for us to see a true picture of God, "full of grace and truth" (John 1:14). But the problem of distortion is still partially with us, for the content of the words we read in the Bible which describe Jesus and the character of God is greatly influenced by our memories and relationships.

HOW THE GOOD NEWS
BECOMES THE BAD NEWS

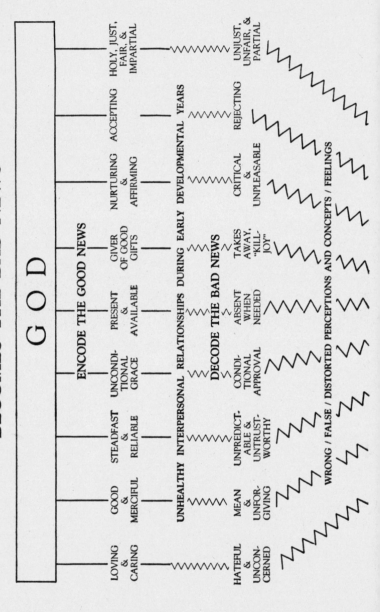

GOD

ENCODE THE GOOD NEWS

| LOVING & CARING | GOOD & MERCIFUL | STEADFAST & RELIABLE | UNCONDITIONAL GRACE | PRESENT & AVAILABLE | GIVER OF GOOD GIFTS | NURTURING & AFFIRMING | ACCEPTING | HOLY, JUST, FAIR, & IMPARTIAL |

UNHEALTHY INTERPERSONAL RELATIONSHIPS DURING EARLY DEVELOPMENTAL YEARS

DECODE THE BAD NEWS

| HATEFUL & UNCONCERNED | MEAN & UNFORGIVING | UNPREDICTABLE & UNTRUSTWORTHY | CONDITIONAL APPROVAL | ABSENT WHEN NEEDED | TAKES AWAY, "KILL-JOY" | CRITICAL & UNPLEASABLE | REJECTING | UNJUST, UNFAIR, & PARTIAL |

WRONG / FALSE / DISTORTED PERCEPTIONS AND CONCEPTS / FEELINGS

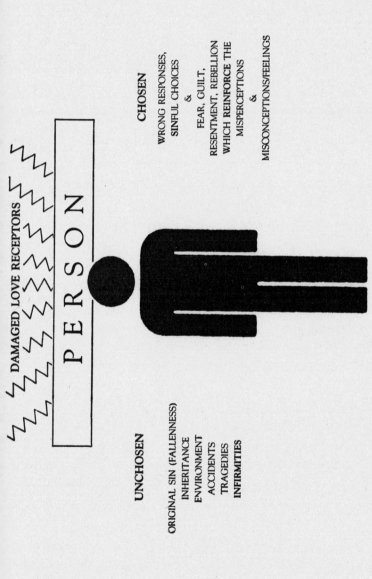

DAMAGED LOVE RECEPTORS

PERSON

CHOSEN

WRONG RESPONSES,
SINFUL CHOICES
&
FEAR, GUILT,
RESENTMENT, REBELLION
WHICH REINFORCE THE
MISPERCEPTIONS
&
MISCONCEPTIONS/FEELINGS

UNCHOSEN

ORIGINAL SIN (FALLENNESS)
INHERITANCE
ENVIRONMENT
ACCIDENTS
TRAGEDIES
INFIRMITIES

WHY THE HOLY SPIRIT SOMETIMES NEEDS A TEMPORARY ASSISTANT
(LIKE A PASTORAL COUNSELOR)

How the Good News Becomes Bad News

Because it is so important for us to understand the connections between what we hear about God and what we feel about Him, I have illustrated the process on the chart. Beginning at the top, you will see the Good News as revealed to us in Jesus Christ. If you have seen Him, you have seen the Father (John 14). While this list of God's characteristics is not complete, it is sufficient to give a true picture of the goodness of God. You will note that the lines coming down are straight. This represents their truthfulness—the truth and grace revealed in Christ.

As you continue reading downward, you will notice that the lines become jagged and twisted. This means something is happening to the straightness and truthfulness of the Good News about God as they pass through unhealthy interpersonal relationships. In every case now, the Good News has become distorted into the Bad News and the person perceives God as the opposite of who He really is. Compare the truth on the chart with the distortion. The loving, caring God has become hateful, or at least unconcerned.

Many times I ask counselees, who have already given me their theological picture of a loving God, how they think God feels about them. All too often they say, "I don't think He really cares for me; I'm not sure He knows I exist. If He does, I'm not sure He's concerned." In contradiction to their theological view, they *feel* that God is mean and unforgiving, holds grudges against them, and constantly reminds them of past sins; that He is a very legal God who keeps accounts on them. As in the song about Santa Claus, "He's making a list and checking it twice!"

Sometimes I ask people who are having a difficult time describing their God to draw a picture of Him. As you

might imagine, I have an interesting collection of draw-
ings. Several depict a huge eye which covers a whole
page—God watching everything they do, waiting to catch
them at some failure or wrongdoing. Others have drawn
angry human faces, or birds of prey with sharp beaks and
talons. One young theological student said he couldn't
draw very well but next time he'd bring a picture of his
God. I was very curious about it. It happened to be the
Christmas season and he brought a magazine with an art-
ist's drawing of an extra large, angry and demanding
Scrooge sitting behind a desk, quill pen in hand with his
debit-credit ledger before him. Standing in front of the
desk facing Scrooge was small, terror-stricken Bob
Cratchett. Pointing to Scrooge he explained, "That's
God," and then to Cratchett, "That's me." And just
think, this young seminarian made an A in his theology
class!

Follow the chart across. Instead of trusting a God who
is predictable in His steadfastness and reliable in His
faithfulness, many Christians are filled with fears and
anxiety because at a deep gut-level they sense God to be
untrustworthy. They sing about "amazing grace," talk
about it in Sunday School, and even witness about it to
others. But on a performance level, they live fearful of a
God who accepts and loves them only when they "measure up." They quote verses about God *always* being with
them, but ask me, "Why is it that God never seems there
when I need Him?" Their God is not, as Scripture puts it,
"the giver of every good and perfect gift" (James 1:17), or
the One who desires to give good things to His children
(Matthew 7:11). Rather, He is a killjoy who delights in
taking from them whatever they really enjoy. "Why is it
that God always seems to take from me everyone I've ever
loved?" It's as if they feel God constantly keeps an eye on

them, and as soon as they truly love someone or are having too much fun at something, He gets jealous and says, "Give it up, or I'll take it away from you."

They do not see God as a nurturing and affirming parent who is always encouraging His children in their development; or as a good father or mother, pleased with every step of growth. Instead His face seems critical and unpleasable. He is indeed the inner voice that always says, "That's not quite good enough." So they feel rejected by God, unaccepted by Him because they are unacceptable to Him and thus caught in the vicious circle of trying to please an unpleasable God. They become POWs—not prisoners of war but Performance Oriented Workers. The final distortion is yet to come, for as I pointed out in *Healing for Damaged Emotions*, these Christians usually have hidden anger against God. Therefore, they come to feel He is unfair and partial in His judgments. He is an unjust God to them, but treats everyone else fairly. This is why they often freely tell others about a loving God and explain the plan of salvation by grace, but are unable to apply it to themselves.

Now we come to the crux of the whole matter. Notice what it was that brought about the twisting of the lines and the distorting of God's character—*unhealthy interpersonal relationships, especially those which occurred during the early development years of childhood and adolescence.* More than any other factor, these faulty relationships cause the emotional damages which distort spiritual perceptions. You will notice on the chart that the twisted lines actually go in both directions. They proceed down from the bad experiences and relationships and also come up out of the persons. This means that what began from outside sources gradually has been internalized. It is now the way they actually perceive other people, themselves, and God.

It's a way of life. We could liken their condition to a kind of spiritual paranoia. Paranoid persons can take the most loving, affirming statements and twist them into insults, rejections, and even threats. In the same way, Christians with *damaged love receptors* can take the Good News and turn it into Bad News. This is why so many of them have an uncanny knack of missing the wonderful promises of God's mercy, love, and grace, and consistently selecting Bible passages which emphasize wrath, punishment, judgment, and the unpardonable sin. Unless Christian workers truly understand the dynamics of this, *they will not be able to help these damaged persons.* They will actually *harm* them, overloading more oughts and guilts upon them by giving them the spiritual disciplines of Bible reading and prayer.

Finally, look at the columns on either side of the person in the drawing. The fact that we may have been victims of painful experiences and hurtful relationships does not excuse us from responsibility. Certainly, there are many *unchosen* factors of life, including our fallen natures which in themselves tend to produce distorted pictures of God. There are other factors over which we have neither choice nor control—our biological and psychological inheritance, our geographical and cultural environment, and the accidents, tragedies, and traumas of life. These make up our unchosens which, in many cases, have caused what Scripture would term our *infirmities*. Infirmities are the weaknesses, the cripplings, the inborn and ingrown defects of body, mind, or spirit. They are not in themselves sins but are, rather, those qualities of our personalities which predispose us and incline us toward certain sins. They are the weakened places in our defenses which undermine our resistance to temptation and sin.

On the opposite side of the figure are the *chosen*—the places where we are responsible. We have chosen to make wrong responses to God and to other people. We have held onto our resentments and bitterness and have deliberately decided to disobey God. This has brought us fear and guilt, and has further reinforced our warped perceptions and feelings about God. So, however much we have been victims of the sins and evil of others, we have also sinned, and we must accept our share of responsibility for our problems. We have much to forgive but we also have much for which we need to be forgiven. Yes, it is a complex picture; but its purpose is not to confuse, but to clarify, to help us discover and be healed of those images and feelings which distort our concepts of God. For, in spite of all our commitment to the most rigorous Christian disciplines, we will never find lasting "righteousness, peace, and joy in the Holy Spirit" (Romans 14:17) until we find a Christlike God, the kind of God who, like Jesus, tells us He no longer considers us "slaves" but "friends" (John 15:15).

Will the Real God Please Stand Up?

This section title is the name of an exceptionally helpful article about clarifying our concepts of God (Joseph Sica, *Marriage and Family Living*, August 1983, pp. 18-21). Mr. Sica traces the different ways children experience their parents during the various stages of growing up. He then lists some of the faulty concepts/feelings of God which can develop.

- The Legal God "keeps an accounting of what we do. He waits for us to step out of line, to trip up, to falter, so He can mark us as losers."
- The Gotcha God resembles Sherlock Holmes and

wears a detective's trench coat and dark glasses. Like a disguised private investigator, He is always following at a short distance. The moment we step out of line, He jumps out of the bushes and yells, "Gotcha!" He is much like the "corner policeman" God J.B. Phillips writes about in his excellent book, *Your God Is Too Small.*

• The Sitting Bull God "relaxes in a yoga position on cotton candy clouds, expecting burnt offerings and homage all day."

• The Philosopher's God, Aristotle's "unmoved mover" of the universe, is withdrawn, cold, and distant. He is much too busy running the galaxies to get involved in our petty problems. As one man described Him, He is silently sitting in His office, studying the encyclopedia, His door closed with a "Do Not Disturb" sign on it.

• I have added another, The Pharaoh God. He is an unpleasable taskmaster who is ever increasing His demands, always upping the ante. Like Pharaoh of old, His commands move from "Make bricks," to "Make more bricks," to "Make bricks without straw." He is the very opposite of the Heavenly Father-God of Jesus. He is more like the horrible godfather of the mafia who always says, "Measure up or else."

Picturing Relationships

Why are these distorted concepts of God so damaging? Think of them in relationship to people. It is a basic principle of all interpersonal relationships that the ideas and feelings we have about people always affect the way we see them and relate to them. Our mental pictures of people determine how we assume they will act toward us, for we expect people to be like our pictures of them. Our pictures also determine how we will act toward them. For example, if I think a person is honest when he is actually a crook, he may cheat me when I trust him. But the opposite can also happen. If I assume he is a crook when he is actually honest, then I become the loser because I won't trust him. In both instances I have lost, and for the same reason—my wrong picture of the person.

If this is true in human relationships, how much more important is it in regard to our relationship with God! Most of our failure to love and trust God stems from our pictures of God as unlovable and untrustworthy. And most of our anger against Him is not really against the true God but against our unchristian or subchristian concepts of God. The only encouraging thing about all this is that God knows and understands us. He is not angry with us for our lack of trust or our anger toward Him. Rather, He is very saddened that our false picture of Him keeps us from getting to know Him as He truly is. He is far more brokenhearted about it than we are. That's why He longs to help us find healing from the hurts which have contributed to the distorted concepts/feelings about Him.

8
DIFFICULTIES FROM THE DISTORTIONS ABOUT GOD

WRONG CONCEPT/FEELINGS OF GOD lead people to various kinds of spiritual problems. Some of these are possible indications of the need for a healing of memories. While many of them are related, it will be helpful if we look separately at some of the most common ones.

The Inability To Feel Forgiven
One of the most precious beliefs of evangelical Christians is called "the witness of the Holy Spirit." This theological term means the inner knowledge and confidence that we are the redeemed children of God. Note the word *redeemed*, for there are two ways in which the Bible speaks of God's children. *All humans are God's children in the sense of being created.* Because God created humankind, He sees no barriers based on race, culture, sex, or educa-

tion. But in another and deeper sense, the Bible is very plain that *not everyone is a child of God*. Jesus Himself described some people as children of the devil (John 8:44). Being spiritual children of God means a totally new relationship with Him and requires *redemption*—forgiveness and new life. Redemption comes about by grace, through faith in what Christ has done for us in His life, death, and resurrection. And the assurance that we have received redemption is given to us by the Holy Spirit who comes to live within us. The clearest Scripture about this was written by Paul: "For you have not received a spirit of slavery, leading to fear again, but you have received a spirit of adoption as sons by which we cry out, 'Abba! Father!' The Spirit Himself bears witness with our spirit that we are the children of God" (Romans 8:15-16).

Like many Christians, I misunderstood this passage for many years. I mistakenly thought this witness was solely the work of the Holy Spirit who overwhelmed and overpowered us with assurance. His witness would be so strong that we just couldn't help knowing and feeling that we were redeemed. But my counseling experiences have made me aware that the verse doesn't say that at all. It says that *His Spirit bears witness with our spirit.* That is, this inner assurance is not simply a witnessing to us, but a witnessing together with our spirits. His Spirit (capital S) witnesses along with our spirit (small s)—the divine and the human working together. This is in perfect accord with the biblical principle that it always takes at least *two* to constitute a true *witness* (Deuteronomy 17:6; Matthew 18:16). So it is the Holy Spirit and our spirits agreeing together which creates inner confidence that we are forgiven and accepted as children of God.

But what if our spirit has been so badly damaged that it simply cannot maintain this witness? What if the receiving and perceiving capacity of our personality is so distorted it cannot think/feel of God as Abba, as Papa? And cannot think/feel that He could possibly call us son or daughter? Because of unresolved and unhealed past experiences with parents, family members, teachers, spouses, or even leaders in the church, many Christians have such poor concepts of God they are unable to maintain an assurance of this kind of relationship with Him. In chapter 1, we referred to the fact that children learn a language of relationships long before they can learn a language of words. And the painful memories of unhealthy relationships often cry out so loudly that they interfere with learning the new relationship with God.

It is a known truth that children learn from the concrete to the abstract, from actual experiences with things and people to thoughts and concepts about them. They only gradually think in terms of abstract ideas as they grow older. So concepts like love, acceptance, faith, justice (fairness), and dependability are based on real experiences with actual people, particularly those people of most significance to them. This combination of concepts and feelings based on relationships is the very foundation for their basic experience of God's mercy, forgiveness, and the witness of the Spirit.

The things we teach our children about God's character are certainly important. We are to bring up our children "in the discipline and instruction of the Lord" (Ephesians 6:4). But, as we have already pointed out, this teaching should be given within an atmosphere and climate where *the experienced character of the parents and other significant adults is consistent with the expounded character of God.* When there has been contradiction between the two, we usually see a lot of emotional and spiritual wreckage and persons with damaged love receptors. These are the ones who find it very difficult to maintain a consistent assurance that they are the loved, forgiven, and redeemed children of God.

Two things are often necessary to correct the damage. *First,* a healing of the primary relationship which caused the problem. With the assistance of a counselor or trusted friend, they need to go back to the hurts which caused the damages and find healing for those memories. This will allow them to break free from the painful pressures of the past. *Second,* they need to develop trusting relationships. This begins by learning to trust the counselor or pastor. But it should continue as they become a part of a new network of relationships with other Christians in the church or small support group. Here they can experience openness and unconditional love and come to believe that they are accepted, even when they are not acceptable. How many times Helen and I have seen the beginnings of this great transformation during a marriage enrichment weekend, when a small group of Christian brothers and sisters have enveloped someone with a kind of unconditional love they have never experienced before. Many of them later testify that it was then they really felt loved and forgiven; this assurance has stayed with them.

The Inability To Trust and Surrender to God
Another common spiritual problem which may indicate the need for memory healing is the inability to trust God and surrender to Him. Much of what we have written about the preceding difficulty applies to this one also. However, an important principle distinct to this inability is that God created us so that we would not trust or surrender to anything we are afraid of. This is a part of a

divinely implanted protection system. In the presence of the dangerous or the fearful, our alert systems go into action. Our bodies produce chemicals which arouse our defenses, and our minds and spirits quicken their pace. This is a God-given survival mechanism, so that we don't go rushing out to embrace snarling bears or hissing cobras. Rather, we hesitate in the presence of that which we are afraid to trust.

This same principle makes it very difficult, if not impossible, for some people to surrender to God. When we ask individuals to trust God and to surrender to Him, we are presuming they have concepts/feelings of a trustworthy God who has only their best interests at heart and in whose hands they can place their lives. But according to their deepest gut-level concept of God, they may hear us asking them to surrender to an unpredictable and fearful ogre, an all-powerful monster whose aim is to make them miserable and take from them the freedom to enjoy life. They believe that if they seek first the kingdom of God and His righteousness, then, "all these things will be *subtracted* from them." This is their inward translation of Matthew 6:33.

Within an emotionally healthy person, there is enough original sin and selfishness to insure a continued struggle in fully surrendering his or her will to God. But we are talking about a deep-seated commitment-anxiety which goes far beyond that. And behind this anxiety is always a distorted concept of God which makes it almost impossible for such a person to surrender to Him. Unless Christian workers are aware of this, they will not be able to lead these damaged persons to surrender, but will only increase their problems by presenting an overdemanding God who always asks them to do what they cannot do and never helps them get over the barriers which keep them from doing it.

You pastors and counselors who are confronted by suspicious Christians who sincerely desire to grow in Christ, but who are held back by this kind of deep-seated commitment-anxiety, need to check out their gut-level concepts/feelings about God. Is He really fit to trust and to love? I often ask my counselees that very question. One man, who was very knowledgeable in Scripture, answered me by reversing Jesus' words in Luke 11:11-12, "I guess down deep I really feel that God is the kind of Father who, when I ask for bread, gives me a stone, and when I ask for an egg, gives me a scorpion." Is it any wonder he was finding it difficult to make a full surrender to a God about whom he felt that way? Or that he was angry and resentful?

When you delve into the reasons for this distorted idea about God, you will usually discover a picture of God that blends with a picture of unfair, unpredictable, undependable and, therefore, unworthy parents or other significant persons in their lives. The memory of painful experiences with them is so strong that they are now unable to trust anyone enough to surrender. If you and your counselee will work together to bring healing from the rejections and resentments surrounding those memories, you will be on the way toward discovering the God who can be respected, trusted, and loved.

Rather than pressuring struggling Christians into saying, "I'll try to trust," it is far better to help them understand and find healing for the true source of their dilemma. Then they can go on to say, "Lord, I trust You with my inability to trust You, or anyone else, for that matter." This is not just a play on words but an important shift in their personal center of gravity. When that center moves from being ego-centered to being Christ-centered,

they have made a good start toward surrendering to
Christ. They are beginning to risk the kind of openness
and integrity which Jesus accepted and honored when He
healed the son of the man who said with tears, "Lord, I
believe; help Thou my unbelief" (Mark 9:24, KJV).

Intellectual Questions and Theological Doubts

The third category of problems which can indicate the
need for the healing of hurtful memories centers in intellectual questions and doubts. You may be wondering why
something so obviously *mental* is included in a list of *emotional* symptoms. As I have already said, Scripture speaks
of persons in terms of wholeness. This is particularly evi-
dent when it comes to our beliefs and doctrines, for there
is a basic unity, an interdependence of the emotions, the
mind, and the will. Within the central citadel of the self,
each one affects the others. This reflects the Hebrew belief that faith involves the whole person—feeling, thinking, and acting. We deceive and flatter ourselves if we
imagine our theological beliefs are purely rational, a matter only of mind and thought. Our religious beliefs are
greatly affected by our feelings and our way of life. Did
you ever notice how illnesses—even something as simple
as the common cold—affect our faith, our prayer life, our
patience, and how we think and feel about God, ourselves, and others? When we move that feeling factor
over into the religious realm, it becomes more intense,
especially when we are attacked by questions and doubts
about the Christian faith. *It is not simply that reason attacks
our faith, but that deep-rooted emotions overwhelm our reason
as well as our faith.* Those emotions are so powerful they
can outvote and overpower our faith. How often have I
heard, "Of course, I know better with my *head,*

but my feelings are so strong I just can't help doubting that God really cares." Yes, in spite of our desperate attempts to cling to the reasons for our beliefs, our emotional scars may still sabotage our theology and fill us with doubts.

The finest book written in recent times on the subject of doubts is *In Two Minds* by Os Guinness (InterVarsity Press). He covers every possible angle of doubt in both a scholarly and a practical way. In a chapter entitled, "Scars From an Old Wound," he discusses those doubts which are purely psychological in origin. He describes the problem so clearly with this beautiful illustration. Picture healthy faith as a person who has a firm grip so he can reach out and take hold of anything he wants to. Now imagine that this person has an open wound in the palm of his hand. The object he desires to hold is in front of him, and his muscular strength is sufficient. But the unbearable pain which will result makes it very difficult or even impossible to grasp the object.

This is exactly what happens to many Christians with unhealed emotional scars. The very process of trying to believe exerts great pressure on an emotional wound that is too painful to bear. In fact, the questions and doubts which seem to be coming from their *heads* are actually arising out of some deeply buried hurts in their *hearts*. Something has so deeply damaged and distorted their concepts/feelings of God that they yield to doubt so they will not have to reopen those painful wounds. William James, the father of American psychology, understood this problem clearly. He claimed that religious and theological doubts which are emotionally rooted cannot be solved by reason. Early in my ministry, I discovered he was right.

Since I have worked near educational institutions for a

large part of my life, people have constantly approached me with various "intellectual problems regarding the Christian faith." Many of these people have been genuine seekers after truth, and I have never hesitated to spend hours helping them achieve a reasonable and defendable faith. But I soon learned to recognize that no amount of biblical study or theological reasoning could dispel the questions and doubts of certain people. Since the doubts were emotionally rooted, even after one aspect of their problem was cleared up, another would arise, and then another and another. I also discovered a fairly predictable list of theological problems which troubled these people, like, "Are the heathen lost?" "Predestination—does God choose only some to be saved?" "How do I know whether or not conversion is simply psyching myself up?" There were also many troublesome Scriptures, some of them the harsher passages from the Book of Hebrews (6:4-8; 10:26-31; and 12:15-17). And, of course, there was that all-time favorite, the unpardonable sin. Did you ever try to argue someone out of thinking he had committed it? If so, you've discovered it's usually a complete waste of time.

With certain damaged Christians, these are not intellectual problems at all, but emotional problems appearing in theological disguise. They are unhealed hurts which are so entangled with their concepts/feelings of God that they have become a part of *the way these people keep from feeling their pains.* As Guinness reminds us, *true intellectual doubts need answers, but emotionally rooted doubts answer needs.* Until those basic, inner needs are met and old wounds healed, the doubts still remain. For it is less painful to bear the pain of the doubts than to face the pain of the traumatic memories of events which caused them.

This is an important area with which pastors or counselors need to be well acquainted. Otherwise, they will try direct and overly simplistic remedies which will not help people but drive them into deeper despair. For these people truly *want to believe*, sometimes more than anything else in the world. This desire is exactly where some of their questionings come from—*they want so much to believe that they cannot stand to risk the terrible pain of believing and then being let down*. For this disappointment is what they have experienced somewhere back in their lives.

For example, can someone who has never experienced any genuine love, but only hate, rejection, and even cruelty as a child, really believe God loves him? Can a son who has gotten nothing from his unpleasable mother but criticism, nagging, correction, and put-downs really believe/feel that he is pleasing to God and that "there is therefore now no condemnation for those who are in Christ Jesus"? (Romans 8:1) Isn't it to be expected that he would gravitate toward some of the more judgmental Scriptures, like the ones from Hebrews I've mentioned?

What kinds of theological questions would you expect from a daughter who said of her father, "I never knew whether I'd get hugged or slugged, and I never knew what made the difference"? Or, the young lady who said, "When Dad went out the door, we never knew when he'd be back—a few hours, several days, or a couple of years"? Or the one who told me with deep sobs, "I just covered my face with the pillow and cried when Daddy would have sex with me"? Without a major healing, can these women really have a proper theology about God as the Heavenly Father who loves and cares for us and will never forsake us?

Yes, these are extreme cases, but they clearly illustrate the point. Not all theological questions and doubts are a sign of disbelief, unbelief, or rebellion. In many instances, they are symptoms of the need for a deep, inner healing.

It is only *after* this takes place that such people are able to reshape their faulty doctrines and properly understand the Scriptures.

Problems with Neurotic Perfectionism

Since I have written extensively on perfectionism in *Healing for Damaged Emotions*, I will not go into great detail here. However, the thousands of letters and phone calls I have received from its readers only reinforce my earlier conviction that this is one of the commonest emotional viruses infecting Christians today. Let us not confuse the biblical doctrine of Christian perfection with its greatest hindrance and counterfeit, neurotic perfectionism. Biblical perfection is a level of maturity and sanctification in which the holiness of Christ is imparted to us by the infilling Holy Spirit, so that we are enabled to live a life of habitual victory over sin. Like our justification, this is purely a gift of the grace of God. It is received and lived by faith, and is basically a matter of relationship. It does not depend on perfect performance (works) but on faith in His perfect performance. Everywhere in Scripture we are admonished to make this level of living the aim of our sanctification. Christian perfection goes by many names, depending on one's theological background. Unfortunately, it is called by some the "Higher Life," or the "Deeper Life," or the "Spirit-Filled Life," but that is because these Christians seem content to live on a lower, shallower, and half-filled level of life. As the norm for all Christians, and because it is God's will for His redeemed children, true Christian perfection is the healthy pursuit of Christian excellence by those who, out of gratitude because they are accepted and loved as they are, want to please God and be at their best, *on His terms*.

Although neurotic perfectionism may resemble what we have just been describing, it is actually the greatest enemy of true Christian perfection. For neurotic perfectionists strain compulsively and constantly to make themselves acceptable to God and to measure their relationship to Him in terms of performance and accomplishment. They are restive achievers, not resting believers. The root cause of this is the concept/feeling of an unpleasable God. Their God is an increasingly demanding tyrant who requires perfect performance. He is a punitive judge who has no tolerance for imperfection. At the slightest failure, He expresses His displeasure and covers them with condemnation and guilt. This leads perfectionistic Christians to twist the truth, so that *they rate their behavior before God higher than their relationship to God.* They place conduct before faith, deeds before trust, achieving before receiving, work before worship, and performance higher than relationship.

It naturally follows that perfectionists have oversensitive consciences and live under "the tyranny of the oughts." They try to placate their anxiety by the false humility of belittling themselves and overemphasizing doctrines and duties, rules and regulations. But even though they constantly try harder, they are guilt-ridden, fearful, and subject to mood swings and depression. This is because the basis of their relationship with God is performance, not grace. At best, it is a Galatian mixture of the two. Many such Christians unconsciously take the very channels of grace—repentance, confession, prayer, Bible reading, and Christian service—and turn them into works. Their attempts to find inner peace and be pleasing to God by reading another chapter, praying another hour, and taking on another job at the church, never succeed. Then they feel caught in a trap from which there is no escape. They are literally "damned if they do and damned if they don't!" This is the ultimate despair of neurotic perfectionists and it drives many sincere Christians to emotional or spiritual breakdown—or both.

To make matters worse, such people often have major problems with loneliness, for their relationships are lacking. Because they are sure that others (like God) will reject them when they discover their imperfectness, they literally beat others to the punch by becoming oversensitive, defensive to criticism, and inhibited in communication. All this, in turn, worsens their relationships with others. They unintentionally set themselves up for the very rejection and disapproval they so much fear. In response to the vicious cycle, their inner voice says disapprovingly, "It's just like I told you—people won't accept you unless you're perfect." The cycle is completed when they then react with anger and resentment toward the others who "ought" to have responded with acceptance and love anyhow. Then everyone is included in their frustration and despair, especially those closest to them.

Christians suffer from varying degrees of the perfectionist virus. There is some of it in all of us because it is part of growing up in Christ. Even those who have been brought up by the best of parents, and in the most ideal of situations, still have to battle wrong concepts of God. Our own sinfulness, both unchosen and chosen, and Satan, the father of lies, will see to that! Perhaps the most amazing thing about the love of God is that *He accepts us in spite of our distorted pictures of Him,* and works with us until we gradually come to know Him as He truly is. Most of us begin our spiritual pilgrimage with a mixture of law and grace. It's only by experiencing His great faithfulness through our many failures that we finally come to the place where we can really sing that line in the hymn,

"Rock of Ages,"—"Nothing in my hands I bring, simply to Thy cross I cling."

However, there are many who, in spite of their moral earnestness and faithful disciplines, do not grow out of perfectionism and into freedom and maturity in Christ. Instead, they continue to be performance-oriented and even sink into the neurotic levels of perfectionism we have been describing. They are very sincere but very unhappy Christians, carrying out their daily duties in quiet despair. If they are parents, they unknowingly create a legalistic, graceless home atmosphere of conditional love which spreads the deadly infection into one more generation. Thank God this does not have to be. They can be cured by experiencing God's unconditional grace at the deepest levels of their being. But this requires right concepts/feelings about God, and is sometimes impossible without a deep inner healing of those memories which have contributed to the distorted pictures of Him.

Mary and Rabboni

Some years ago a lady named Carrie came to counsel with me following a sermon I had preached on the need some Christians have for inner healing. She was a very intelligent, attractive, Spirit-filled Christian, and highly successful in her profession. During the sermon, the Holy Spirit had pulled back a veil so that she became aware of a deep anger against God. Since Carrie was in her fifties and had been a diligent Christian almost all her life, this came as a great shock to her. We counseled regularly for several months, slowly working through many layers of repressed emotions until finally the Spirit led us to the place which needed healing. The memories returned slowly, going all the way back to when she was about ten.

It was during World War II, and Carrie's favorite brother was in the army. One day an army officer came to the door and delivered the terrible news of the death of her brother. Carrie's parents were devastated, her mother going to her room to shut herself up for days. Carrie literally had to take over. She had to be the strong one and shoulder many of the household responsibilities. *She never had a chance to express her grief over the loss.* She loved that brother more than anyone else in the world, and though she was hurting badly, no one cared enough to listen to her sorrow. Into her crushed and overloaded heart crept an anger against God for allowing her brother to be killed, and against her family for never allowing her to express her tears. She had to become a ten-year-old superwoman whose needs were totally unmet.

Now, with these painful memories, came a chance to express her grief. But there also came the realization that because of what had happened then, she had become a closed person, rather perfectionistic and overdemanding in her outlook. The core of her anger and pain was this, "I've always been forced to do and be someone I'm really not." And this had carried over to the way she perceived her superiors *and God,* who always seemed to be pressuring her into being more than she really was. With Carrie's permission, let me share her letter which describes the turning point in her healing.

> After talking with you yesterday, I came home for lunch and, as I usually do, reached for a book. I've been reading in *Rabboni* (by W. Phillip Keller) and had reached the chapter "The Forgiveness of God." Without really thinking, I started to read. Suddenly, it was not just a book, but God was using it to say, "You're for-

given." It seems incredible, but for the first time in my life the reality of being forgiven came home to me. I haven't words to express the song that began inside—the wonder of feeling forgiven and free.

The realization of forgiveness came as a result of thinking on your answer to my question, "What do I do now?" Your reply, "Do nothing," seemed too simple; yet finally the truth came home that that was the exact answer I needed, for God had already done it. There may be lots of reprogramming ahead, but today I think it will happen, for I'm finally on the road.

This was indeed the beginning of a new road of grace and freedom in her life. Like Mary in the greatest recognition story of the Bible (John 20:1-16), Carrie found her Rabboni, her Master, in a new relationship.

Perhaps it would be fitting to close this chapter with a prayer from St. Augustine, who early in his Christian life faced the problem of a wrong concept of God.

Should I call on You for help or should I praise You? Is it important to know You first before I call on You? If I don't know who You are, how can I call? In my ignorance, I might be calling on some other object of worship. Do I call on You, then, in order to know You? . . . It's settled: let me seek You, Lord, by asking for Your help in my life.
(*The Confessions of Augustine in Modern English,* Sherwood E. Wirt, Zondervan, p. 1)

9

PREPARING FOR THE PRAYER TIME

Up to this point we have been laying the foundation for the healing of memories. Now I will begin to describe the counseling and prayer sessions and the manner in which I conduct them. In this way, I hope the final chapters can become a kind of manual for both counselors and counselees who desire to use this special form of spiritual therapy. Since the prayer time is the very heart of it, this will be described in considerable detail in the next chapter. But first, let's look at some ways to prepare for it.

Preparation of the Counselee
It is very essential that counselees be properly prepared for the time of prayer. To rush into it without really knowing what needs to be done, and what the real issues are, is to practice magic, rather than to participate in a miracle, as it should be. God is not a respecter of persons, but He is a

respecter of conditions and principles. He works through the laws of the mind and spirit. Indeed, there are certain principles which govern healing and prayer itself. That is why, in almost every situation, there must be a time of counseling which precedes and follows the prayer sessions.

At the very outset, I explain to people that I will probably be giving them homework. This makes them aware of the fact that no one (not even God) can help them without their consent and cooperation. The picture of the Holy Spirit helping us with our infirmities (Romans 8:26) is one of participation on our part with the One who "takes ahold over on the other side" of our problems. The purpose of homework for counselees is to help them get in touch with the repressed memories and feelings which are causing them emotional and behavioral problems. At the heart of all remembering is association, for associations are the links which cause our minds to recall experiences. By remembering one picture, we then recall another, because our minds have somehow associated the two. When the memories are clearly recalled, there is a strong possibility of reexperiencing the emotions which originally accompanied the experience. The reverse is also true. That is, if we can experience certain feelings, there is the possibility the memories associated with those feelings will reenter our consciousness.

It will help us at this point to recall some of the findings of Dr. Wilder Penfield, the world-renowned Canadian neurologist. Beginning in 1951, Dr. Penfield did years of extensive research on the brain and memory. He began with the fact that the whole nervous system uses a very slight amount of electrical current to transmit its sensory information to the brain, and the brain in turn uses that current to record and store the data. He experimented by stimulating the memory areas of the brain with small amounts of electricity and discovered that every experience we have ever had is recorded in minute detail by the brain. Whether or not we can consciously recall them, they are still stored in our memories.

Even more important for our study, *the feelings which went along with the experience are also recorded in the brain.* In fact, they are recorded in such a way that they cannot be separated from the memory of the experience itself. So, remembering is more than just repicturing or recalling. *It is more accurate to speak of it as reliving an experience.*

Penfield went on to show that because of this capability to relive experiences, we humans can function on two psychological levels at the same time. We can be conscious of living in our present surroundings now and, *at the same time,* so vividly be reliving a previous experience that we feel as if we are living in the past. This is why memories have such power over us and furnish us with so many of the concepts and feelings of our present experiences. We not only remember what we felt, but we tend to feel the same way now.

The purpose, then, of the preparation time, is to help the counselees bring into their consciousness both the pictures and the feelings of those painful memories which they have partially or totally pushed out of their remembrance; to help them see, hear, feel, and understand what they experienced and to bring it before the Lord for healing. I don't mean to be facetious in saying that if Penfield accomplished this by electrical impulses, surely the Holy Spirit can also do it if we ask Him to. And so, through reading, listening to tapes, and opening our hearts to Him in quiet meditation and prayer, He can reawaken memories and enable us to become aware of those painful experiences which are interfering with our growth in Christ.

Reading and Listening Assignments
After several conversations with counselees, if I sense
God leading me toward this form of inner healing, I suggest certain reading assignments. What I recommend depends largely on the problem areas with which they are
struggling.

To help people open themselves and become aware
of hidden hurts, I have found these books most helpful:

Your Inner Child of the Past, Hugh Missildine, Simon
and Schuster

The Art of Understanding Yourself, Cecil Osborne,
Zondervan

Healing for Damaged Emotions, David A. Seamands,
Victor Books

The Key to a Loving Heart, Karen Mains, David C.
Cook—especially helpful to women, because it is written
about the home.

The following books apply to specic areas of need:
• Concepts of God
Your God Is Too Small, J.B. Phillips, Macmillan
May I Hate God? Pierre Wolf, Paulist
Putting Away Childish Things, David A. Seamands, Vic-
tor Books
• Guilt, Low Self-Esteem, Depression
Happiness Is a Choice, Minirth and Meier, Baker
Guilt and Grace, Paul Tournier, Harper and Row
Free for the Taking, Joseph R. Cooke's great book on
grace, Revell
• Relationships with Parents
Cutting Loose, Howard Halpern, Bantam
• Struggles over Forgiving Others
Healing Life's Hurts, Dennis and Matthew Linn, Paulist
Forgive and Forget, Lewis B. Smedes, Harper and Row

Healing Where You Hurt, Jon Eargle, Bridge Building
Ministries
- Incest and Sexual Abuse

A *House Divided,* Katherine Edwards, Zondervan
- Homosexuality

The Broken Image, Leanne Payne, Crossway Books
- Grief and Loss—General

A *Grief Observed,* C.S. Lewis, Seabury
- Death of a Child

But for Our Grief, June Filkin Taylor, Holman
- Miscarriage or Stillbirth

Empty Arms, Pam Vredevelt, Multnomah

Some people find it more convenient or beneficial to
listen to tapes. They can do this while driving to work or
in the evenings in the privacy of their homes. I have
found tapes to be extremely useful in helping people become aware of their needs. A catalog of my own cassettes
is available from Tape Ministers, Box 93396, Pasadena,
California 91109.

Writing Assignments

As people read books or listen to tapes, they should keep
notes of whatever thoughts and memories come to them.
The important thing to remember is this: *nothing is too
insignificant or seemingly stupid and silly to record.* For
though it now looks stupid or petty from an adult stand-
point, at the time it was very important and brought deep
hurt. Perhaps the most painful part of the memory is at
that very point—the significant others involved in the
incident didn't realize how much it meant and that's what
hurt the most! Whatever comes to mind, as one reads or
listens, should be jotted down. Sometimes it is very pro-
ductive to keep a diary or journal during this period.

For counselors who would like to learn more of this technique, I would highly recommend Morton Kelsey's book *Adventure Inward: Christian Growth Through Personal Journal Writing* (Augsburg).

Ways of Getting in Touch with Our Emotions

The real purpose of the homework assignments is to help people become aware of the true feelings connected with their repressed memories. The most subtle trap to avoid in this whole process is "the paralysis of analysis." This is where it all turns into a great big *head trip*. It is possible, through an extensive time of counseling, for counselees to very clinically describe an extremely painful past. They can analyze it all in their heads, realize the problems which need solving in their heads, and work out the solutions in their heads. But after it's all over, they will discover that nothing has really changed. It was all a kind of fascinating intellectual and spiritual game. *Everything took place in their heads, but their hearts and ways of living were untouched.*

I do not mean to downgrade the place of the mind in our healing. We have consistently stressed the biblical idea of the whole person, and this certainly includes our minds. There must come a time of reprogramming our thoughts and transforming us through the renewal of our minds. With some Christians, it is possible to go directly to this and help them realize their full potential of life in Christ. But with others, Christian workers need to realize this cannot happen until they are first freed from their emotional hangups. When we tell such damaged persons the only thing wrong with them is "wrong thinking" or that they should "stop living in the flesh and claim their rightful life in the Spirit," all we do is increase their guilt and deepen their despair. I have spent many hours picking up the pieces for disillusioned Christians who have been pushed into trying this shortcut. *It simply will not work, not because of any lack of desire on their part, or lack of power on God's part, but because God cannot violate His own principles in bringing them to wholeness and holiness.* As in the case of the lady described in chapter 8, their deeply buried negative emotions must first be brought into the light and dealt with.

Therefore, I again want to stress the importance of tapping into these submerged feelings. Many people are terribly afraid of doing this; fearing they will lose control of their emotions, they keep it all on a head level, always wanting to analyze. "But I want to know *why . . .*" is a phrase they will use over and over again. All this does is to reinforce their defenses and drive their real feelings even deeper into the concrete of their personalities. That's why, when we give counselees their homework, we must constantly emphasize the importance of allowing feelings to come to the surface.

Through the years, my counselees have taught me many important truths. They have suggested methods of reviving hidden memories and frozen feelings. On one occasion, I gave a young lady the usual reading and writing assignments. Before we met again she went home for the holidays. While she was there, the Spirit prompted her to go through all the old family pictures which were stored in the attic. She decided to arrange all her pictures in chronological order, beginning with the earliest baby photos right up to the present. It was fun to do—for a while, until she began to discover a rather pronounced change in her pictures. What began as pictures of a cheerful baby and continued as a happy little girl started to change. The difference in her posture and facial expressions was markedly different. There was a kind of furtiveness and sadness in her face.

As she laid out all the pictures side by side, wondering about the difference, she began to tremble with a strong sense of anxiety and fear. Memories she had pushed out of her mind for years forced their way back in. We had not been able to clarify them through the counseling process. Now they began to sort themselves out and she was able to pinpoint some very painful experiences of sexual abuse by a lesbian baby-sitter. Because of this visual experience through pictures, it did not take long to lead her to the place of healing, when she returned for counseling. Ever since then I have suggested to others that they look at old photos, family pictures, and high school or college yearbooks. This use of pictures has proved very helpful in situations where we were unable to push memories back to where the real hurts originated.

Taking journeys to places associated with painful memories can also bring back buried emotions. Former hometowns, schools, even churches connected with painful memories, can all be used by the Spirit to bring pain to the surface. One divorcee, filled with great guilt and self-despising because of her past life, told me she had gone back to the very place out in the country where, as a teenager, it all began. She said, "I drove out by myself and parked the car where we had parked that night. Then I got into the backseat where I first threw away my self-respect. And there, on the backseat of the car, I sobbed it all out and asked God to take the burning sting out of these memories."

Today, as the lovely wife of a pastor, she has a very special ministry to hurting teenagers and young divorcees who are trying to find a new life. She is truly one of God's healed helpers!

The Counseling Sessions

While there is much that can be accomplished by those who take their homework seriously, it is usually not possible to find full healing by oneself. The divine principle of healing—confession to one another and prayer on our behalf by another (James 5:16)—emphasizes the need for a counselor's help. Look once again at the figure in chapter 7. Since unhealthy, destructive relationships of the past have distorted some people's sense of perception, it stands to reason that healthy, constructive relationships in the present are necessary to restore a proper sense of perception. This is why a healthy trust relationship with a counselor is often absolutely essential.

I define a counselor as a *temporary assistant* to the Holy Spirit. Both of the italicized words are important. *Assistant,* because the goal of all Christian counseling is to assist people to become emotionally and spiritually mature enough to relate directly with the Holy Spirit, the Great Counselor. *Temporary,* because dependence on the counselor should never become permanent. If it does, then the counseling itself becomes a part of the problem and not a means of solution; a part of the disease, not the cure. It is only a *temporary* means to an end, the goal of total dependence on the Spirit. However, this in no way underestimates the crucial importance of counselors in the healing process. All through history God has used humans as assistants, not only to carry out His work, but also to "stand in the gap" as His intermediaries who show people what His character is really like. There are vast numbers of people who feel like the scared little girl whose mother was trying to comfort her with the assurance of God's presence. "I know that," she said, "But I need a God with skin on Him!" The counselor fills this need. For many counselees, this is the first time in their lives they have

131

experienced a stable, trustworthy, and truly loving (accepting yet confrontive) relationship. Thus the very *being* of the counselor is the commencement of healing.

But the *doing* is also of great consequence. This is not the place to go into detailed instructions of the *listening process* involved in this procedure. Those who find themselves in the role of counselors—pastors, Sunday School teachers, various church workers, or trustworthy friends—must develop the art of listening. Fortunately, it is a learned art and can improve as we practice it. We've all had the experience of simply listening to someone open their hearts to us and then tell us, much to our surprise (since we hardly said anything), "Thanks so much; you've been a great help to me." What we need to remember is that perhaps no one ever cared enough or valued their opinions enough to listen to them before.

Your listening should be *perceptive,* listening with your eyes as well as your ears. Watch for those signs of body language—tearful eyes, sighing and swallowing which literally push rising emotions back down into their hiding places, as well as blushes and blotches on the face and neck. Listen for "motor mouths," those who use talk so that they won't be able to feel anything. There is also the nervous laughter which is so incongruent with what is being described. It can be disrupting; but remember, it's really a very hopeful sign. That kind of laughing means people are getting in touch with some deep emotions and they don't know what to do with them. Laughter is the one acceptable American emotion. "Brave kids never cry," and are often not allowed to express any negative emotions. But they can always laugh, even when "they are crying on the inside." Don't be afraid to gently confront people and help them become aware of the impressions you are receiving. An important part of their self-awareness is *understanding the meaning* behind what they say and do.

Again, your listening must be *prayerful.* While carefully concentrating on what is being communicated to you, at a deeper level you must be using your spiritual radar to *tune in to the discernment of the Holy Spirit.* In addition to the sensitivity of your own spirit to the human spirit sharing with you, you must be prayerfully receptive to the inner voice of the Divine Spirit. Remember, however, that you are a fallible human being and need to handle the impressions you receive with great humility. Some people think they have an infallible "hot line to God," and use their impressions too quickly and bluntly. I often have to remind myself of the time when a layman dropped by to see the great New England preacher, Joseph Parker, and found him pacing the floor of his office. "What's the trouble, Doctor Parker?" he asked. Parker replied, "It's really very simple: *I am in a hurry, but God is not!*" You need to be in prayerful alignment with the Spirit, but also be willing to "test the spirits" (1 John 4:1) to see if the impressions are really from Him. I have discovered that *the hasty thing is usually the wrong thing.*

On the other hand, after careful and prayerful consideration, do not be afraid to obey His leadings. Many times I have felt the Spirit was helping me discern what someone's real problem was, even though they had not directly mentioned it. And when I finally shared it with them, although this was often quite painful, it proved to be the place which actually needed the most healing.

Playback, Role Play, and Coaching
Many pastors and laypersons will be called on to assume the role of counselor. What I write here is intended to

help such nonprofessionals who can be very important links in the healing chain. The preparation counseling for healing of memories demands all the human wisdom and skill we can possibly acquire, plus the discernment of the Spirit. This is because we are often attempting to help people to remember things they really don't want to remember, and to face pain they have long been trying to avoid. So in addition to careful and prayerful listening, our responses can be very decisive in the process.

Counselees are often unaware of what they are really saying. Counselors shouldn't always directly tell them what they are hearing. Instead, they should help them become aware of the true meanings behind what they have shared. In this way, counselees will also become aware of what they are feeling and thus be able to pray much more fruitfully.

When counselors pick up important clues, they should learn the *playback* technique of feeding it back to the counselee so that he hears it the same way. In chapter 11, I have included the story of Larry's healing. This illustrates the use of careful listening and playback in helping people recognize hidden needs.

Role play is another way of helping people reach feelings. Such questions as, "What would you have liked to say to him/her if you'd have had the chance?" or "What did you really feel like doing, if you'd had the opportunity?" If it's a matter of what they would like to have said, it is much more effective to ask the counselee to act as if you are that person and to say it directly to you. Their tendency will be to keep it all in the third person—"I would like to have said . . . ." Try to guide them into speaking directly to you, or possibly to an empty chair in which the person involved is supposedly sitting. Thus, "Dad (Mom), I wish you would listen to me when I try to tell you what I'm feeling," or "(Person's name), I am feeling very rejected by you."

Role play cannot be forced on people but should flow naturally from the conversation. It can be a powerful tool in helping people realize what they were actually feeling during the original situation. Often they are surprised at the rush of painful emotions which comes out while they are speaking. I once lost a few buttons off my coat when a counselee got carried away by the anger generated through the role playing, but the results made it worthwhile!

We must keep constantly *coaching* for memories, meanings, and feelings. They are all important. They all need to be *owned* before they can be *disowned.* This is simply the psychological way of stating the same truth we talked about in chapter 5—we cannot confess to God what we do not first acknowledge to ourselves. It's amazing how tenaciously people will deny their feelings because "Christians are not supposed to feel that way, especially not *Spirit-filled Christians.*" This is denying reality and is a form of untruthfulness. Until it is brought up and out into the light, it cannot be healed by the One who is called the Spirit of Truth.

This emphasis on becoming aware of true feelings is not just some modern psychological "feeling therapy," which brings about an emotional catharsis so that people will feel better. It is the bedrock scriptural reality of confession, repentance, and forgiveness. The word *confess* comes from the Old English words *con* and *fess.* To confess is simply to *fess* "say or speak" and *con* "along with." To confess is to know and say along with God what God already knows and says about certain things in our lives. This is what we are helping people do through our counseling times. We are helping them know the truth which makes them free through insight and awareness. Better still, we are helping them to know the Son who in redeeming and healing power will make them free indeed! (John 8:32, 36)

The Final Assignment

When it is agreed that everything has gone as far as it can by sharing together and by the kinds of homework we have described, the counselee should be asked to do the final assignment. From all that has been discussed and prayed over, let the counselee make a list as the guide for the prayer time. This list should include the most painful and recurring memories which have been seen as causing the main emotional and spiritual hangups. These do not need to be written out in great detail; just a brief phrase or sentence for each item is enough, so that it will be remembered and prayed over. The list should be as specific as possible, in the sense that persons be remembered by name, and incidents or attitudes and atmospheres be listed specifically. One man called it his "hit list." When I asked him why, he explained it this way, "Because those are all the people who hurt me so much I hate them and want to hit them for it." Although he may have overstated his case, I think he had the general idea of what the final list should include. Counselees should bring their lists with them. The list should also be undergirded by prayer for a spirit of willingness to follow the Spirit's directions during the prayer session.

The Preparation of the Counselor

When the counselee is ready, it is time for the counselor to prepare for the crucial time of prayer.

First, counselors should review all their notes—what they have jotted down during the counseling sessions plus any ideas and impressions which may have come to them while praying for the particular person.

Second, they should spend time in meditation and prayer, asking the Spirit to give them emotional and spiritual empathy with the counselee. They need to become so one with them in prayer that they will actually participate in their pain, feel their sufferings, and "bear their burdens."

After this prayer for empathy, they should then exercise faith for the healing of their counselee. Faith has been called a form of "sanctified imagination." This means we pray using our imaginations to visualize people as healed and freed from the painful chains of their past; that we picture them as changed and made new, as whole persons in Christ.

Finally, counselors should pray for the emotional and spiritual energy necessary for this time of prayer. Once, after healing a woman, Jesus spoke of virtue going out of Him. Baron von Hugel writes of "the neural cost of prayer." Every counselor knows how tiring and draining a difficult counseling session can be. But that doesn't compare to the energy required to walk people through a healing of memories prayer time. It is a very exhausting experience for both parties. Counselors should ask God for the extra physical, emotional, and spiritual strength necessary for this experience. Believe me, they will need it!

10
CONDUCTING THE PRAYER TIME

BECAUSE THE PRAYER session is so important, it is essential that it be planned properly. The session requires *unhurried time* and *an unpressured schedule*. This means that it should not simply be an hour worked into a regular counseling schedule. It should not be subject to clock-watching by anyone. The pastor or counselor should not be anxious about some other person impatiently waiting for an appointment, or a committee meeting that is about to begin. To allow for this kind of freedom, I always schedule at least a two-hour block for the prayer session.

I want to go through the memory healing process with you, step by step. I will describe the prayer session in detail, instructing, explaining, and illustrating as if we were actually going through it with a counselee who has been adequately prepared.

The Opening Explanation

Begin by explaining or reminding the counselee about the concepts of prayer which are basic to memory healing. Remind him or her that Jesus Christ is Lord and, therefore, the Lord of time. (See the section, "Accept Christ as a Present Helper," chapter 5.) Describe how Jesus will be walking back into time with you and dealing with the situation as He would have, had you asked Him at the time. Once more clarify the reason for this—"The real problems are not with the adult, the grown-up person you are just now. So we need to reach back into the past and let Jesus deal with your child in those places which need the actual healing. This is because you seem to be stuck or hung up at those particular places of hurt. So far as possible, I want you to talk to God as if you are now the child (or young person, or adult) you were at that hurting place in your life."

Next, explain, "We will be using a very free-flowing conversational type of prayer. We will just talk to God as openly as we have been talking together. Nothing fancy, no windups or closings, just talking to Him as if He's sitting right here with us.

"I am going to feel free to interrupt your prayers if I feel you are getting off target—like being too negative, telling God how bad you are. Or, I may point out some new insight or discernment from the Spirit.

"And you should also feel free to stop in the middle of the prayer to look at your list, to ask a question, or share something the Spirit has reminded you of, something you have not recalled until now."

If distorted concepts of God are a real part of their problem, try to assist the visualization process by helping them find their most comfortable picture of God. Since they are going to be talking very personally to God, this is an important matter. Strange as it may sound, I often ask people which will be easier for them, talking with *God* or with *Jesus?* In most instances they will say something like, "I feel better with Jesus; I guess I'm scared of God." Or "Jesus is okay, but I can't stand God." Once in a while this is reversed, "I don't know, Jesus seems too near, *a little too real.* God seems farther away, a little safer, I guess."

If there have been unhealthy and harmful relationships with parents, avoid using the term *Father* for God, even though that is your usual way of praying. I will long remember a prayer time with a lady who had been a victim of incest. Toward the end of the hour, she suddenly began to address God as "Heavenly Father." She stopped right away, burst into fresh sobs and said, "Oh my God, You know that's the first time I've ever been able to call You that!" Sometimes it is best to use a more or less neutral term such as *Lord*; but I have discovered that most of the time, people are comfortable with imagining a picture of Jesus for this prayer time.

Make clear what the content of the praying will be. They are to tell God what they have been telling you, not hesitating to look at their list, if they feel it necessary. They should make sure they tell God what they are feeling as they relive the experience they are describing—that is, what the child, teenager, or young adult was feeling at that time.

The Counselor's Opening Prayer

I always open in prayer. Though there is no set format, that prayer will usually contain words something like this:

"Lord Jesus, we quiet our hearts before You at this time. . . . We know that You have been in on all our conversations, so You know all the things we have talked about. We're glad You understand us even better than we understand ourselves.

"We need Your help now because we don't know exactly how to pray. But You've promised us in Your Word that at times like this You will send Your Holy Spirit to actually come into our hearts and to pray in us and through us; and even when we don't know exactly what to say, You will take our sighs and groans and pains and translate them into prayers. We ask that You will do that right now—come into John's/Mary's heart and pray for him/her. Give him/her the very words to pray and awaken the very feelings he/she needs to relive.

"Now, Lord Jesus, I want to bring before You a little ____-year-old boy/girl named_____. He/She wants to talk to You about some things which have caused a lot of pain. I know You are going to listen. So I bring You

_____.

"Now,_____, just talk to Jesus and tell Him whatever is most on your heart."

The Counselee's Prayer Time
Usually it won't be long before the counselee will start praying. However, if there is a long pause, be prepared to wait it out patiently and prayerfully. If the hurts are very specific, counselees will usually begin with some of the earlier incidents of childhood. If it's more a matter of atmosphere and climate, they will often begin with later general impressions and then move back to the specifics. However, this is completely up to them—whatever is uppermost in their minds is where they should start.

It is impossible to regularize or formalize this prayer time. This is one reason why many counselors are afraid to get into memory healing—its direction cannot always be controlled and its contents cannot always be predicted. Frankly, it can be somewhat frightening, and counselors must simply "hang loose in the Spirit" and be ready for almost anything.

Sometimes, it takes quite a long time for counselees to really open up in prayer. You should not hesitate to interrupt and redirect their praying, if you feel they are being too general and thus trying to avoid facing painful issues. Even during the prayer time, make every effort to help them relive the original emotions.

Coaching and encouraging are perfectly legitimate. Statements like these are appropriate and helpful: "Why don't you also tell Jesus what you were feeling when that happened?" or "Don't be afraid to let the feelings come up and the sounds come out as you talk to God about that." Or, if it seems they are struggling to maintain tight control over their emotions, "Don't be in a hurry: let's just stay with that memory for a while and let our emotions plug into it. I have the feeling there is a lot of unexpressed pain in that one." If there is a rush of feelings with sobs and tears, wait patiently, praying silently in your heart. This time when the counselee shares his deepest hurts with the Lord is extremely important and *should never be rushed.*

Sometimes, if the Spirit imparts a deep sense of discerning empathy, you should feel free to enter into the very prayers of the counselee by praying *as if you were the counselee, and using the editorial we.* For example, "O Lord Jesus, You know how *we* felt, *we* really wanted_____ to die," or "*We* felt so ashamed and guilty *we* wanted to kill ourselves," or "Lord, *we* were really angry at You, the fact is *we* hated You for taking Mother away from *us*—she was all *we* had." This approach often gives the counselee the courage to face their bitterness against God or someone else they are supposed to love, and to verbalize it openly.

At other times, if there is a lull in the counselee's prayers, it is helpful to clarify issues and emotions by asking such questions as, "What are you sensing to be the real issue in this? What was it that hurt you so much and made you so angry?" Or, "I'm sensing there is more involved than_____. Is there a word or feeling that the Spirit is giving you about this?" Here are some of the words counselees have given in reply:

abandoned	shamed	worthless
totally alone	dirty	desperate
annihilated	unjust	hopeless
panic-stricken	trapped	wiped out
like garbage	rejected	betrayed

Don't be surprised if, when counselees reexperience a situation, they revert back to that time. Their voices may become like those of children, and they may say and do things appropriate to that stage of life. They may also express in words now what they weren't able to (or allowed to) then. Like, "Mama/Daddy, please don't leave me, or (hit me), or (do that)."

Questions can also come pouring out—addressed to the people involved then, or to you, or to God, such as,

"How could he/she have done that to me?"

"Why did they adopt me when they didn't really want me?"

"Where was God in all this?"

"How could they do that when they said they loved me?"

"How could I have ever done such a thing?"

"If I could only understand why!"

144

Questions represent many different things. They may
be an attempt to figure it all out, so it can be kept controlled on a purely intellectual level, so the pain of it
never has to be faced. Or questions may mean the expres-
sion of the deepest kind of feelings—*great anger* against
God, others, and self, or the *sheer agony* of not being able
to comprehend how such painful experiences could ever
happen in the first place.

When New Memories and Insights Emerge

One of the most amazing experiences which can happen
during the prayer time is the emergence of the heretofore
unremembered. You may hear comments like this: "I just
can't believe it, I had never remembered that before." Or,
"It's amazing. Up till now, I could never remember anything before I was ____ years old, and now all those things
have become clear to me." The new insight can be one of
the most important results of this prayer time. This is
where the Holy Spirit literally prods us with His divine
electrodes, somehow interjecting His light and power into
the synapses of the nervous system and bringing to conscious recall those memories which have been forcibly
stored in some deep layers of the brain/mind. No wonder
the Spirit is described in Romans 8:27 as "He who search-
es our hearts" (NIV). Here is a supernatural work of the
Spirit, the Great Counselor, who is able to open our
hearts (subconscious minds) to ourselves. Many times during the counseling sessions, the counselee and I have both
started down a certain path of felt need. Then, while
praying, some new or enlarged memory has emerged to
become the means of showing us a different trail which
ultimately led to the true place of healing.

George came seeking help for the usual syndrome of

emotional and spiritual problems accompanying perfectionism. He was oversensitive to the approval or disapproval of others, generally angry and impatient with the faults of "professing Christians." He never felt quite acceptable to God and was often troubled by fairly severe depression. We agreed that God had graciously helped him find the right kind of wife—warm, accepting, and understanding. But, as is often true of perfectionists, that was part of his problem—he found it difficult to accept this affection and love, though he truly loved her and desired to express that love more than anything else. During counseling he shared several incidents when, as a supersensitive child, he had been deeply hurt and had begun to draw back from people. One harmful experience kept troubling his memories. As a lad in his preteens, he found a lot of his dad's hidden porno magazines. When he confronted his parents about them, his mother became very angry, but his father just laughed at him. Later his mother talked to him about it in private. She put down his dad and lectured George about sexual evils, hoping he would never become "a dirty-minded man like his father." When George made out his list, this was one of several hurting memories he had written down. In prayer, we took up the childhood hurts and he forgave his peers and others whom he felt had rejected him. When we began praying about the porno incident, he was able to forgive both his parents for their part in it and to receive forgiveness for his long-held resentments against them.

During his prayers, however, he recalled other things which turned out to be the real memories which were affecting his present life and marriage. For he had repressed the fact that he looked into those magazines, was sexually aroused, and felt very "dirty" about it. His mother's lecture drove this feeling even deeper underground.

This began an attitude in which, unable to accept his own teenage sexual development, he had become very prudish about sex and had assumed an extremely critical and self-righteous attitude toward others. He suddenly remembered the cruel and unchristian way he had treated a pregnant teenager during high school. She had looked to him as a Christian friend, desperately seeking his help, but he had rejected her in very pharisaic fashion. He then remembered several other incidents like this and began to see the true nature of his judgmental and critical perfectionism. He also realized why he was unable to accept and enjoy his wife's love and intimacy—he had been clinging to a false sense of prudish moral superiority, thinking he was thereby a better Christian than she was. With these new memories and insights, we were then able to pray at the place of real damage and receive deep healing. It only took a small amount of follow-up and reprogramming on George's part to bring about a marked change in his spiritual and marital life. And it was all made possible because the Spirit searched out some repressed memories during our time of prayer.

Letting Christ Minister to the Past
As we have already stated, the uniqueness of memory healing is walking back into our past with the Lord and asking Him to heal us at a specific time and place of need. In the first two chapters of my book, *Putting Away Childish Things,* I wrote of this in general terms and gave several illustrations of Christ's ministry to the "hidden child in us all." This is where counselors can be at their best as temporary assistants to the Holy Spirit. For it is during such prayer times, after counselees have shared their most agonizing memories with God, that we as

counselors can most helpfully mediate. Our prayers should be to Jesus, asking for His direct intervention and healing presence. We should ask Jesus, whom we believe is present with us in the memories which are being relived, to minister to the counselee for their particular need at that time.

For example, let us suppose a counselee has just told God about some extremely painful experiences of rejection. In the incident there is deep humiliation and the person is left feeling stupid, worthless, and unloved. The counselee is filled with emotions and stops praying to weep.

This is the perfect time for the counselor to pray, using the imagery of Jesus blessing the little children: "Lord Jesus, You who took the little children in Your arms, do that now for _____, one of Your children who is hurting so badly. Let _____ sit on Your lap and put Your arms around him/her. Tell _____ how much You love him/her and how sorry You are that he/she hurts so much. Let him/her feel Your approval, and know how pleased You are with him/her."

Another beautiful biblical picture of Jesus which is so helpful for such times is the Good Shepherd. You can pray, "Lord Jesus, You who are the Good Shepherd promised to take the little lambs in Your arms and give them Your protection and love. Do that just now. Let _____ feel your arms around him/her in warm and tender care. Like a good shepherd washes and binds up the cuts and bruises of his lambs, wash his/her wounds and pour in Your healing balm."

The basic idea behind this imagery is to match the particular aspect of the character of Christ to the specific needs of the counselee at that time. So, for feelings of rejection we visualize the One who knows what it's like to

be "despised and rejected of men," and who went out of
His way to care for people's needs. If counselees are over-
come by the terrors of loneliness and abandonment, we
picture the Christ who understands us, since He was forsaken by all His disciples, and who even experienced
what it's like to not be able to feel God's presence, as He
cried out, "My God, My God, why hast Thou forsaken
Me?" Christ understands this feeling of loneliness so well
that He promises never to leave us abandoned or
orphaned.

When they are filled with the confused emotions which
accompany memories of sexual abuse, or the guilt and
shame of sexual sins, we imagine Jesus in all His purity.
He is pure but not prudish, sinless but not censorious. For
painful childhood experiences, we ask for Christ's tender
and pure embrace; for the whisper of His assurance which
restores a feeling of purity. For experiences in which they
bear responsibility, we pray for His arm around their
shoulder and His noncondemning words of forgiveness.
We spend time kneeling beneath the Cross, receiving the
washing and cleansing which restores feelings of virtue
and self-respect.

For those struggling with torturous memories of unpleasant parents, teachers, and disapproving Christians,
our prayers should picture Jesus lifting them from their
groveling position until they are standing tall and straight
before Him. Then we listen as He says to them,
"_____, you are My beloved son/daughter, in whom
I am well pleased!"

We have only scratched the surface of the possible application of this principle of "imagineering"—visually
matching pictures of specific hurts with pictures of His
special healings, based on His actual ministry as presented
in the Gospels.

Forgiveness—The Heart of Healing

We come now to the subject of forgiveness which is the very crux of the healing of memories—forgiveness in the sense of *forgiving and being forgiven*. It would be impossible for me to exaggerate its importance in the healing process. It is at this point where the greatest struggles of prayer will take place, and where counselors will expend the most spiritual energy. It is also here where counselors will be most sorely tempted to give up; for that very reason, this is usually where the battle is won or lost. Let us take a closer look.

There is no question that forgiveness is the key relational issue in the Bible. This is true for all our relationships—with God, others, and ourselves. We often speak of grace and of our salvation being unconditional. This is true in the sense that there are no *conditions of merit* we humans can meet. There is nothing we can do in order to *earn* or *achieve* God's grace. It is given to us freely as the gift of His love.

But in another sense, forgiveness is conditioned by our response. It is still unconditional, because the very ability to respond depends on His grace. Without that prevenient or preceding grace, we would not be able to say either yes or no to His offer. But God has so created us that forgiving is basic to our responding to His gift of grace. It would seem He has made us so that unless we truly forgive others, we make it impossible for Him to forgive us. Not impossible in the sense that He withholds His offer of forgiveness until we first forgive; no, for in one sense, as Paul states in 2 Corinthians 5:18-19, God has already forgiven our sins through Christ's death on the Cross and offers us His forgiveness freely. It is impossible because He has made us psychologically so that we are not able to *receive* His forgiveness unless we forgive.

This is plain throughout the entire New Testament, and is the one condition our Lord stressed again and again. In His model prayer, in Matthew 6:12, He stated, "Forgive us our debts, as we also have forgiven our debtors." And in His commentary on this prayer, He explained, "For if you forgive men for their transgressions, your Heavenly Father will also forgive you. But if you do not forgive men, then your Father will not forgive your transgressions" (Matthew 6:14-15).

In Matthew 18:23-35, we have His parable of the unforgiving servant, which ends with the angry master turning the culprit over to the jailers for torture. Jesus then made this application of the story, "So shall My Heavenly Father also do to you, if each of you does not forgive his brother from your heart." In Mark 11:25, Jesus once again set a condition when He said, "And whenever you stand praying, forgive, if you have anything against anyone; so that your Father also who is in heaven may forgive you your transgressions."

It is clear that God has built this supremely important principle into the very structure of all interpersonal relationships. It is based on the nature and character of God Himself; and since we are made in His image, it has been built into us. So we are talking about a basic biblical and psychological principle. Every experience of memory healing of which I have been a part confirms this. If we want forgiveness without forgiving, we are asking God to violate His own moral nature. *This He cannot and will not do.*

The essentiality of forgiving is the reason I have put so much stress on being honest about feelings. For the first step toward forgiveness is *to acknowledge feelings of resentment and hate.* When people experience severe hurts, they usually end up hating the persons who caused these hurts. *If they then bury the hurts, they also bury the hates.*

But God has so structured our personalities that we cannot do this and get by with it forever. We cannot long ingest and integrate hidden resentments, anymore than our stomachs can digest and incorporate bits of broken glass. In both, we are going to feel a lot of inner unrest and pain! Both require serious operations. The healing of memories is a form of spiritual surgery and therapy.

My Personal Experience of Inner Healing

In order not to hurt anyone, I have had to wait until both of my parents were gone before I could share the details of my own healing. I was born in India of Methodist missionary parents who gave forty years of service there. My mother died in 1981. Dad was ninety-two when, on his twelfth postretirement "shuttle-service" visit to India, in 1984, he fell ill and died. He is buried in his beloved India. I will always remember our final week together when I flew out to be at his hospital bedside and have "closure" with him. It's impossible for me to say how much I owe to him. His saintly life as my earthly father certainly made it easy for me to believe in my Heavenly Father.

But Mother and I were a different story. We were both nervous, high-strung personalities, and from the very beginning found it difficult to get along together. I remember my childhood struggles with ambivalent feelings toward her, feelings I was never able to express or share with anyone. We came to the States when I was eleven, and a year later my parents returned to India, leaving my brother and me in the good care of a loving grandmother. Mother was far away, so getting along was no longer a problem. A conversion experience in my early teens brought many changes in my life. I felt I had dealt with my resentments, and my new life in Christ gave me a much better attitude toward her.

I had always suffered from asthma. In my teens it grew worse until, by the time of my freshman year at Asbury College, it became so serious I was unable to take my spring quarter exams. In spite of many prayers on my behalf, the asthma continued and I accepted it as a handicap I must learn to live with. By now I was a committed, growing Christian, and during my college days I entered into a deeper experience and life in the Holy Spirit. I also strongly felt the call to missions. So together with a lovely college classmate God had brought into my life, four years, two degrees, and one child later, we left for India as missionaries.

Our work went well for the first ten years. Then one day when I was thirty-four, I was reading a book by Glen Clark during my devotions. The Holy Spirit made one sentence from the book leap out at me. It said that some forms of asthma may be caused by resentment toward parents. I stopped short. Could it be possible? During the next hour, the Spirit peeled off a layer of my mind and I began to remember some deeply buried resentments against Mother. They were specifics I had not dealt with; in fact, I had not even really recalled them for years. The Spirit also showed me that I had not faced some of my true feelings toward God. You see, I had been separated from my parents when they got stuck in India during the early years of World War II. They had left me at twelve and I did not see them again until the morning of my twentieth birthday. And after all, it was God who had called them to be missionaries in the first place. Oh, I had spiritualized it all, basking in the glow when people would say, "Isn't it wonderful, your parents are missionaries!" The gut-level truth was that I felt angry about those lonely teen years. All my friends had their parents with them and places to go on holidays.

For the next few days, I shared some of these thoughts with Helen, and we talked and prayed about them. I forgave and was forgiven. And I experienced a cleansing/healing from my resentments at a deeper level than I'd ever known before. But then came the serendipity. How truly gracious God is! In the midst of the struggle, we had forgotten all about my asthma. But God hadn't, and He gave me something I never even thought to ask for. Can you believe it? I've never had a wheeze of asthma since then!

I always hesitate to tell about this, for fear some may jump to conclusions about their own physical ailments. I cannot make generalizations from my particulars. I can only share my experience with you and trust the Holy Spirit to guide you into the truth of what He has in store for you. The main reason for sharing my personal experience is to emphasize the central place of forgiving and being forgiven in the healing of memories.

Important Ingredients for Forgiveness

During those days of prayer and struggle, the Spirit dealt with several aspects of my resentment-forgiveness problem.

• First, I had to take a look at some of my very specific hurts and be willing to relinquish all feelings of resentment. Was I holding on to a secret desire to get even in any way? At first I thought to myself, "Of course not." For by then I had learned from relatives some of the tragedies of Mother's life—an alcoholic father who had spent a few years in prison, and some other painful childhood traumas. I could explain the causes of many of her neurotic problems; but *explaining is not the same as forgiving.* We may trace all sorts of fancy psychological schemes about those who hurt us and not face the fact of our resentments against them.

Finally, I realized where my real problem lay. Of course, I understood her background and therefore I would forgive her. But first, *"Let me just once tell her all the ways she has hurt me. I just want her to know what she's caused me to feel—that's all."* This is a most subtle form of resentment—a way of wanting to get even. The Spirit asked me to turn that over to Him. Some counselors believe and teach there can be no true forgiveness unless we *always* go at once, confess our bad feelings to the person(s), and attempt to bring about *immediate reconciliation.* I believe this is a dangerous teaching and I have seen much hurt come as a result of it. God has His own perfect timing for this kind of resolution, *if it is ever to come about.* With some individuals, like Joyce Landorf's *Irregular People,* it may never happen. God asks us to give Him our complete willingness for reconciliation, but the timing is His. My first struggle was to fully and unconditionally forgive.

• Then the Spirit brought a second aspect to my mind. From then on, I would assume full responsibility for who I was and what I did. Up to that time, I had the most wonderful, built-in excuse for all of my failures. It worked automatically, like the doors which open as we go in and out of a supermarket. Whenever I failed in any way—in my ministry, marriage, or spiritual life—that automatic excuse-making gadget inside my mind went on, and a sign read, "You failed because you had that kind of a mother. If only she hadn't done that to you, you would have been okay; it's her fault, not yours!" Wow, it was the most comforting device! You see, it guaranteed that I (that is,

the true me) had never really failed. With this built-in
device, I was able to maintain my perfectionistic, unreal
superself intact. If I gave it up, what would happen to
me? The Spirit was relentless, "Remember, if you really
forgave her, then that gadget's gotta go. From now on,
you alone are responsible." Frankly, this was more difficult
than the first issue.

• Then a third matter emerged, and for me, it was the
hardest of all. Way back in a closet in my heart, I had
hidden a secret bargaining point, a place of leverage with
God. If I really forgave, stopped my scapegoating, and let
her off the hook, then surely God would see to it that
somewhere in the future she would give me the affection-
ate love and affirmation I had never received from her.
Surprise! The inner voice of the Spirit was gentle but
firm, "Can you relinquish that possibility? What if you
never get that from her? What if she is never able to give
you that kind of love? Are you willing to accept her and
love her just as she is, even if she doesn't change a great
deal?" This was an agonizing surrender for me. It was
almost as if the Lord was asking too much this time.

Later, when I began to observe similar struggles in my
counselees, I understood what was really at stake. *I was
really trying to offer my forgiveness and love in return for the
guarantee of a promissory note.* But just as God offers us
unconditional forgiveness, so we must give it to others.
Paul's great words in Ephesians 4:32 helped me the most,
"And be kind to one another, tenderhearted, forgiving
each another, just as God in Christ also has forgiven
you."

Finally, standing beneath the Cross, I found the grace
to surrender all claim on the future—for that too was a
form of unrelinquished resentment. Then I was to give my
forgiveness in the same way I was seeking to be for-

given—freely and fully.

• Let me add a fourth fact which I learned later, during the reprogramming stage. Forgiveness, like most matters related to our spiritual growth, is both a crisis and a process. The few days back in India were the crisis point, when, by an act of my will, I obeyed the Spirit and forgave. But there were many, many times afterward when the old feelings returned, or when I remembered some new item on the "hit list," and ancient feelings came alive. The crisis of forgiving really means committing ourselves to be willing to continue the process, whenever it is necessary.

I discovered that resentments are like all other human feelings—they are unpredictable and sometimes they can strike us when we least expect them.

In this respect, feelings of resentment are much like feelings of grief. I have mentioned the death of our first son while we were in India. Ten years later, I supposed all emotions of grief were gone. But one furlough while on a mission deputation trip, I walked into the kitchen of a minister's home. His wife was standing there holding a little blond-haired boy who looked very much like our son. Before I realized it, I started crying! None of us had ever met before and the poor lady didn't know what in the world she had done to cause such a scene. I was embarrassed and had to explain my strange behavior. I had just been completely ambushed by feelings which I didn't know still existed. A similar ambushing can take place in relation to resentments.

Forgiveness often needs to be reiterated. It is far better to be perfectly honest with God when we are struggling with old resentments. It is better to tell Him frankly if we are unable to surrender them and find it impossible to change our feelings. Frankly, I'm not sure we can ever change our feelings. What we can do is admit this to God, and then give Him our willingness for Him to change them.

Our prayers in this regard should be something like this, "Lord, I am sorry for my feelings of resentment and hate, but I just don't seem to be able to change them. So I give You a permit to change them. I *will* not to resent any longer. When the feelings return, I will keep turning them over to You. I don't want to keep having these feelings, and if You will give me a new set of feelings toward the offending people, I will exercise them. So I forgive completely, and ask You to change my feelings."

When we do this, and keep determining *not* to feel resentful any longer, we are surprised how quickly God can change our feelings. We should explain this to our counselees so that when old feelings ambush them, Satan will not be able to accuse them into condemnation and defeat.

I want to emphasize again how crucial it is to lead counselees to the place where they can actually pray, "Lord Jesus, by Your grace I forgive. I surrender all my desires to ever get even in any way. I relinquish them completely into Your hands." Don't underestimate the battle at this point. Counselees may say bitterly, "But I can't, I just can't forgive them. I was hurt too much." You may then need to talk something over on a deeper level; but, as soon as possible, get back to the place of prayer. You are truly wrestling with principalities and powers. Only the Holy Spirit can win the battle. So, persevere in prayer until the grace to forgive is given.

The problem with some counselees is that they have made their hatred a part of their very personalities. They have built their lives around these hatreds and find it difficult to relinquish them. I remember a young college student who shared at great length all the hurts she had received from one of her parents. She truly had a lot to resent and she used her capacity to the full. After considerable prayer along these lines, she suddenly jumped from her chair and cried out loudly, "But I can't give up my hate, I can't give it up. *It's all I've got!*" And though we talked and prayed for a long time, she did not give it up. After she graduated from college, I lost her in the passing parade of students. About fifteen years later, I was preaching in a distant city. A lady came up after the service, told me who she was, and asked if I remembered the time we prayed together about her hate. I assured her I had never forgotten her and had often wondered what happened to her. She replied with great sadness, "I want to tell you, you were right. After two divorces and a nervous breakdown, I'm beginning to realize I should have given up my hate."

Helping People Forgive Themselves

Sometimes the greatest battle is not in forgiving those who have hurt us, or in receiving God's forgiveness for our hates, but in trying to *forgive ourselves.* This is another area where we need to "pray and faint not." Here again, counselors must emphasize the will to forgive ourselves, and the commitment to continue doing this. Direct prayers should be made in this regard. Do not hesitate to ask people, "Will you right now ask God to give you the grace to forgive yourself? To abandon your strange desire to have higher standards than God does? Will you give up your right to condemn yourself? Will you ask God for the grace to never again remind Him of things He says He doesn't remember?"

When a counselee seems unable to do this, I believe

counselors should exercise the authority Christ gave us, in Matthew 18:18-20. We Protestants have reacted against the Roman Catholic misuses of the confessional and the granting of absolution by priests. In doing so, we have given up one of the greatest privileges of our priesthood—being temporary assistants to the Spirit as His instruments to bring forgiveness. There are some people and some types of sin which require humans to mediate a sense of forgiveness. There are two great means of grace open to us, Holy Communion and the laying on of hands. I often use them with people who are struggling with being forgiven or forgiving themselves. I always keep the consecrated Communion elements on hand for this purpose. I have seen forgiving grace break through in miraculous ways as people partook of these sacred symbols. Again, and only with counselees' permission, I may lay hands on them. In prayer I claim the authority given to us by Jesus Himself, "Whatever you shall bind on earth shall be bound in heaven; and whatever you loose on earth shall have been loosed in heaven" (Matthew 18:18). After asking them to agree with me in prayer (v. 19), I close with "And therefore, (name), receive healing," or "Be forgiven," or "You are forgiven, in the name of the Father, Son, and Holy Spirit." If it seems appropriate, I often end the entire session with some prayers of thanksgiving for the healing God has given. If possible, counselees should join in such prayers.

Closing Words and Scheduling a Follow-up Session

After the time of prayer, before you let your counselee go, you should do two things. Schedule a definite follow-up session for not later than a week or two. We shall discuss this in our final chapter.

Then—I learned this the hard way—you should give some words of caution. This has been an emotionally draining experience. It's as if a high caliber gun has been fired, and an emotional kickback is possible. Or, it's as if something has been taken away from the counselee and they may have withdrawal symptoms. They may even experience genuine physical symptoms—a very severe headache, nausea and vomiting, diarrhea, or terrible fatigue. It is possible for a woman to start her period off schedule. If they are completely exhausted, let someone else drive them home. None of these things may happen, but it is much better to warn them of the possibility—forewarned is forearmed.

Stress the fact that their negative feelings are often unreliable and may give them a hard time for a few days or a week. Suggest they give time for those feelings to settle and more reliable and positive feelings to take their place. Also suggest they back away from further pursuing what has been prayed over, and just allow the Spirit to heal them at a deep level. Remind them that the healing of memories doesn't mean they no longer remember things. It only means that the sting and pain have been removed from these memories so that they no longer have compulsive power over their lives. Relearning and reprogramming will now be possible, and you can work together on that, beginning with the next session.

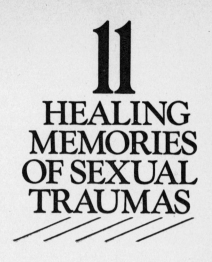

11
HEALING MEMORIES OF SEXUAL TRAUMAS

THE FAMOUS SOCIOLOGIST, Vance Packard, described our present moral atmosphere as a "sexual wilderness." When someone asked why he didn't use the term "sexual revolution," he replied that in a revolution people at least have some goals and know where they are going; whereas today, we are lost, wandering in a wilderness, not knowing where we are going. Every pastor and Christian counselor would confirm the accuracy of his description. In March 1983, Karl Menninger, the respected elder statesman of psychiatrists, said that in the United States incest is becoming almost as common as shoplifting. There is a sharp rise in the statistics for sexual molestation of children and teenagers, as well as for unmarried pregnancies, rape, and incest. We must add to this the rise of the gay culture. Gays are taking advantage of the breakdown of morals and the breakup of families. Many vulnerable youth, confused about their sexual identity because they have never had adequate parental models for masculinity or femininity, are being led down the path of least resistance into same-sex relationships.

All this brings to counselors an increasing number of persons who need healing from the agonizing memories of sexual traumas. Truly we live in a sex-saturated society. Those who involve themselves in the ministry of memory healing must be adequately prepared to deal with the sting and the stain of these sordid memories. It is not an easy ministry. We cannot truly help such people from a distance, protected by the armorplate of the pulpit, any more than we could lift someone out of a cesspool without getting our hands dirty.

Years ago, when I first started my present kind of ministry, a wise old counselor said to me, "Seamands, there are two topics which will always walk into your counseling room—*God and sex.* No matter how hard you try, you can't keep them out for long." It didn't take me long to discover that he was right. What took longer was to find out something even more important—*unless people come to terms with both of them, they can never be fully at peace with either one!* And in many instances this requires a deep healing of damages from past experience and a determined relearning of distorted present attitudes.

Probing Without Prying

No secrets are more carefully guarded or deeply buried in the dark cellars of the soul than sexual secrets. I am constantly amazed when people say, "I've never shared this with anyone before." I wonder how they have kept their sanity and how, at last, they have found the incredible courage to risk telling it. Here is where counselors must cultivate the art of creative listening at its highest. After long experience, some counselors develop a sixth sense that something which is sexually painful needs to be shared by the counselee. But we must be extremely careful to probe gently, to suggest, encourage, and lead *without prying.* We know what they are going to tell us, but we must not tell them we know. We must assure them it will be all right if they tell us and that we will accept them if they do or if they don't. This is done more by an attitude of spirit than by direct statements. People can sense our attitudes; they can spot a censorious spirit from a mile.

What will help bring people over the line to where they are able to share? When they can sense that *we are suffering with them.* How often I have asked a counselee why he didn't share this with his pastor or a Christian worker I knew was close by. The answer invariably is, "Oh, I just couldn't; they wouldn't understand," or, "They'd be shocked. I know what they'd say." I've had people come when I was almost certain what they needed and wanted to share. But they'd beat around the bush for an hour and never quite make it.

Watch and pray; wait and pray; listen and pray; probe and pray. But don't push and pry. It's supremely important they freely choose to share with us. In doing this they have begun the process of healing. Once they say something aloud in our presence, they can never deny it as fully to themselves again. They have offered a very important part of themselves to us that deserves our most tender and empathetic handling.

The Conflict of Contradictory Emotions

There are many reasons why sexual memories can be painful. The first is that *our sexuality is at the very heart of our identity.* Our masculinity or femininity is deeply wrapped up with who we are and how we view ourselves. Damage to this area is bound to deeply affect our self-esteem.

The second reason is that *sex is such a very powerful emotion.* It is so strong that God's plan allows several years of growth and development before the onset of puberty. In this way our bodies and emotions become mature enough to handle these powerful feelings. One of the most terrible facts about child molestation is the awakening of such overwhelming emotions at such an early age and under such frightening conditions. It could be compared to what happens when you try to operate an extremely high voltage electrical appliance through a small extension cord. The wires overheat and eventually burn out. In a similar way, sexual molestation produces an emotional short-circuit which can cause serious sexual damage.

But perhaps the most important reason these memories are so painful is that *sexual feelings can be the most contradictory emotions we humans experience.* We need to help counselees understand their own confusion and turmoil over their sexual traumas. What they have undergone can result in their experiencing sex as an incredible combination of desire and dread, pleasure and pain, fascination and fear. In one and the same emotion we can find a contradictory combination of compulsive longing and guilty contempt. This is why unhealed sexual traumas carried into married life often produce a terrible inner conflict of wanting sex but hating it at the same time.

When Connie and her husband came for marriage counseling, I couldn't help being impressed by them. They had so much to build on—a strong and intelligent Christian faith, fulfilling jobs, and many common interests and activities they genuinely enjoyed doing together. There was only one thing they didn't enjoy doing together—making love. Well, not exactly, for the truth of the matter is that they did. It was what Tim called "Connie's weird reaction afterward" that troubled them both. In fact, the more Connie enjoyed it, the angrier she got at Tim afterward. Connie agreed, "I just don't understand it. Sometimes I seem to go berserk. I've actually struck out at him, right after I've felt the most loving toward him."

She had read all the good Christian books on marital sex; she knew it was a gift from God, and she wasn't inhibited. After a few sessions with Connie by herself, we both began to understand her seemingly strange reactions. She had never shared it with anyone before—especially not Tim. When she was about eight years old, one of her teenage brothers began to involve her in sex play. They "never went all the way, but everything but." This had continued off and on for several years. "At first I was terrified. I didn't really understand it and felt very guilty. He kept me quiet by bribes and threats. Mother had a serious heart condition and he said if she found out about it, she might have a fatal heart attack, and I'd be the one who had killed her. So I kept mum. Later on, I just accepted it. And then . . . " Connie fell silent. I waited. "And then . . . " Silence one more. Connie hung her head and reached for more Kleenex. She did her best to turn on her automatic choke, but she just couldn't hold back the sobs *and the anger.* She got up and paced around the room. "Why that's terrible!" she cried out. "That's awful, I can't believe I could do that. Yuk! That's disgusting." I inquired very gently, "What was, Connie?" I was fairly sure I knew what she was going to say, but I was also sure that *she was the one who needed to say it.* I waited, praying silently back in the subterranean sanctuary of my soul. Finally the words came out in a hoarse, bitter voice, as if she had struck herself across the back with a whip, "I began to enjoy it." She moaned out the rest of it, "What kind of a person am I? With my own brother! I hate him for that, and yet I got so I wanted him to do it."

What was the real issue here? Why her "weird" and contradictory behavior? Where did she need the deepest healing? Of course, she needed to forgive her brother and surrender her hate for him. But the real issue was forgiving herself for getting to the place where she enjoyed it, in spite of the fact that she hated *it* and *him.*

Before we were done, we discovered a whole series of concepts/feelings which needed healing. They were all producing deep inner conflict because they were inherently contradictory and thus pushing her toward her strange love/hate sex life. She knew in her mind that sex was a good gift from God, but she was angry at Him about that too—couldn't He have thought of some other way? She liked men and was attracted to them; but she felt angry at herself for not being "strong enough" to do without them.

Most harmful of all, she loved her husband and needed the affection and joy of intercourse with him. But she was angry at herself for needing him, and therefore angriest at him whenever she showed her deepest need of him and joy in him. Sound confusing? Of course. It is. When Connie finally understood all this, she was able to forgive and be forgiven. She could then forgive her brother for being a sinner and forgive herself for being a human and begin to thank God for His gift of sex. It wasn't long before she and Tim were able to have a really fulfilling marriage.

Centering on the Real Hurt Which Needs Healing

It's so easy to be thrown off the track when dealing with people's sexual traumas. Of course, the actual sexual part is important. Remembering and sharing the specifics and their agonizing emotions is absolutely essential. But many times the mere catharsis of getting it off one's chest will not by itself bring sufficient healing and permanent change in behavior. As in Connie's story, there is often something at a much deeper level which needs greater healing, and it may be quite different from the directly sexual part of the memory. Counselors and counselees need to be very aware of the intricate intertwining of these hurts and make sure they are all dealt with in the healing process. The following three incidents bring out this truth.

• Nobody believed her. Gwen came to talk about a variety of problems. Some were her own; others involved her relationship with her husband. We discussed a great many things, including some distorted concepts of God and grace. Finally, as I had been rightly warned, sex too walked into the office. There were some problems regarding her responses during their lovemaking. These were by no means as serious as some people experience, when an unseen shutter from the past comes down and blocks the free flow of sexual feelings, but serious enough to prevent their marriage from being all they both wanted it to be.

A lot of hurt centered around something that had happened when Gwen was about eleven or twelve years old. She had gone to spend the night at the home of one of her best friends. At about two in the morning she was awakened with a start. Big Brother, who was in his late teens, had crawled in bed with her and was fondling her. Gwen pushed him away and let out a scream. Soon all the lights went on and the household was awake. Of course, Big Brother ran back into his room, pulled the covers over his head and appeared to be fast asleep. The girlfriend and her parents tried their best to calm her down, but Gwen was almost hysterical as she blurted out the story. Finally, the parents called Gwen's parents. They explained that Gwen must have had a scary nightmare and couldn't seem to get over it. It would probably be best if they'd come and take her back home for the rest of the night. Her parents arrived in a short time and Gwen went home with them.

This kind of incident is extremely common and can certainly be very terrifying to a sensitive girl of that age. It appeared to be a rather straightforward matter and the memory which needed healing quite obvious. But when we began praying about it, the real issue emerged. What was the real hurt which had caused Gwen so much pain? More than the shock and bewilderment of what Big Brother did was the fact that nobody believed her—*not even her very own mother and dad.* They too had accepted the nightmare explanation. Oh, how their words still burned and rankled in her memory—"After all, Dear, they are such a fine family and he's such a nice boy. You know he wouldn't do a thing like that. You must have had a terrible dream. We all have those sometimes and they seem so real we think they actually happened."

There is nothing more humiliating to children than to not be believed. It is one of the greatest hurts they can endure. In their eyes it's sheer injustice. They are desperately telling the truth, *but the people they want to be most truthful with are accusing them of telling lies.* Gwen felt so put down by this, so enraged. It began a whole series of unhealthy responses, particularly to her mother. Her anger also started her on the path to a picky perfectionism. So there had to be an inner healing and follow-up (spiritual chemotherapy) for a kind of cancerous growth made up of injustice, sexual trauma, rage, and critical perfectionism. Thank God His Spirit is able to heal and to continue healing. Not so long ago I received this letter from Gwen:

> It's been ten years since my many visits to your office. Many times I wished I could share with you the joys and sorrows, the growing pains and victories that have happened since. A letter cannot adequately give all that was involved in my "reprogramming." So many times I wanted to turn the clock back and never begin—that is, never start the healing. But I always was a fighter (maybe you don't remember) and the positive side of my perfectionism won over! The best part is that over the years God has used me in very much the same kind of ministry to others. We have seen the same needs everywhere, even in other parts of the world.
>
> Hopefully, next year I will get my M.A. in counseling with a concentration in gerontology. Maybe I'll see you in my office someday—Ha! (Author's comment—not very funny!) If you ever travel in our direction, our home is yours. Our little David A. is growing up. He's precious.
>
> Yours in Jesus,
> Gwen

• Smothered by love. Larry was a minister in his twenties. Not only was he single, but he told me again and again he had no interest in women. In fact, though he lived near a beach, he said he had never had any sexual

feelings toward girls. Instead, he felt attracted to mascu-
line men. However, he had strongly repressed such feelings, especially since he had become a Christian at
around age fifteen. He had tried dating young women and
two of them had fallen in love with him. They had initi-
ated the normal courtship, with hugging and kissing. But
Larry had been so uncomfortable with this kind of intimacy that he had broken up with them. Now he had stopped
dating completely—he was too afraid he could never meet
a woman's demands. What brought him to me for help
was an incident in the pastorate. A lonely teenage boy he
befriended had begun looking to him as a father and
spending a lot of time with him. Sometimes he would
even stay overnight at the parsonage. Larry became very
frightened by the growing strength of his homosexual feelings toward the youth and realized he needed to seek help
before he did something which would destroy his
ministry.

No one can really say for sure what causes homosexuality. It seems to be a form of learned behavior resulting
from the interaction of a complex set of varied factors.
However, among the more common contributing elements we often find a family pattern like Larry's—an extremely possessive, domineering mother combined with a
passive or estranged father. Larry's father had openly fa-
vored his more athletic son, while being quite antagonis-
tic to Larry and his intellectual and spiritual interests. His
mother had been overprotective and overaffectionate.
Larry was embarrassed as he shared with me her smother
love—asking him to sit in her lap when he was a senior in
college, getting into bed with him early in the mornings
and hugging him, sitting too close to him while riding in
the car. To be sure he did the right thing, she wouldn't
let him make decisions for himself. On several occasions

when he made a mistake in public, she cried and scolded him because he had "hurt her feelings." I couldn't help noting how many times Larry said disgustedly, "You know it's strange; so often she treats me more like a girlfriend would than as my mother should. She's always telling me how handsome I am and what beautiful eyes I have. And the way she holds my hand when we're in the car or walking down the street really humiliates me."

I was unable to get Larry to become aware of how truly angry he was with his mother. She had done so much for him—and he was too good a Christian to feel such anger!

And then an interesting event took place. Larry was involved in a friend's wedding. During the ceremony he had experienced some strange and overwhelming feelings. This is how he described it to me the following week. "When the couple were taking their vows, I suddenly realized I could never get married; I could never say those vows to a woman." When I asked him for the reason he gave me this fascinating reply, "Because I could never marry another woman when my mother was there watching me."

I could hardly believe my ears! Then I realized Larry was completely unaware of what he had said. Very gently and hesitantly I asked, "Larry, I didn't quite understand. Would you tell me what you said again?"

Once more he replied, "I could never marry another woman." I waited. He still didn't get it. I decided to try the playback method. So I said, "Larry, I want you to hear exactly what you are saying. Take it slowly and repeat those exact words one more time." He went over them slowly, word by word, "I . . . could . . . never . . . marry . . . another . . . " and he stopped midsentence. There was a long pause in which the silence was deafening! Then Larry began to turn red. It was as if he were a transparent glass being filled with tomato juice. The bright redness began at his neck and slowly climbed up to his face and forehead. He was so filled with rage I thought he was going to burst right then and there. We just sat in silence for quite a while, because he couldn't talk anymore. Then, we agreed on an appointment a few days hence. I gave him one simple assignment, "Larry, just allow yourself to feel all your anger against your mother; and as things come to you, write them down."

When Larry returned, he told me of three rage-filled days. As he remembered it all, the whole picture became clear. All his life his mother had used closeness, love, protection, and affection to completely possess him and get whatever she wanted. Though he was extremely angry, he was also so excited by his discoveries he could hardly get them out fast enough, "I just can't explain what's happening to me. But I can now forgive my mother and can let her go. *I can become a man and not feel guilty about it any more.* I can live an independent life. For the first time I can imagine myself married—even sexually—to a woman!"

Then he told me he had gone to a restaurant and met a girl he had known but never really noticed before. His face was glowing. "I talked with her and enjoyed it. I was attracted to her. Her face was pretty; and when I noticed her figure, I actually got stirred up. Before this I was afraid women would manipulate me and control me, and I resented them. Now I feel free to admire them and enjoy them."

By then I was excited. "Larry, do you think you might ask her for a date?"

But Larry was ahead of me. He laughed, "Doc, I already have. I've got one for tomorrow night!"

There were times of prayer in which hurts and hates

174

were washed away. Reprogramming followed, but the change had been so tremendous that our work was easy the rest of the way. Within two years Larry met and married a fine Christian lady. Together they are serving the Lord in a most fruitful ministry. Larry writes occasionally and each letter reiterates his total healing and how happy he is in his married life.

I wish all my counseling experiences with people battling homosexuality were that dramatic and simple. They certainly are not. Some of them are the most difficult I face. They require long hours of counseling, healing, and the help of a Christian support group before genuine transformation takes place.

I have shared Larry's story to emphasize once more the main point of this chapter: when dealing with sexual matters, *make sure that you discover the real issue which needs facing and healing.* So often the sexual injuries are closely intertwined with hurts which originate from a different area. There can be no lasting healing and change until those memories are uncovered and adequately dealt with. The real issue is often the association and relationship between the two. In order to accomplish this, you need to be sensitive to the discernment of the Spirit.

• The betrayal of love. Brenda and I had spent many hours counseling together about many deep hurts inflicted on her by her family. They ranged from an abusive mother, who had once injured her so badly she required hospitalization, to a father who had tried to rape her when she was in the first grade. Our preparation completed, we began a long time of prayer for the healing of these and other stinging memories. Up to now she had described in considerable detail the physical pain she had suffered. Since she was so young, the sexual molestation was especially painful. She had talked about this aspect many times and it seemed to be the heart of the matter. But during the prayer time her voice grew louder until she was almost screaming between sobs, "Oh Mama and Daddy, how could you do that to me? I loved you so much. And I still do." The deepest pain was not physical; it was the agony of being betrayed by someone she loved. *In many sexual traumas, the key issue is the betrayal of love and trust.*

Vangy was a young mother who came for help because of various sexual maladjustments in her marriage. She had been to a secular psychiatrist who, after listening to her story, was convinced she had been sexually molested as a girl. Vangy denied it, saying she could not remember. The psychiatrist explained how the mind is capable of blocking out memories too painful to bear. However, she was not convinced and came to see me saying, "I've got to hear that from a Christian counselor before I believe it." I assured her it was perfectly possible and showed her my files on the subject. We studied in detail the story of the repressed memory of murder, told in chapter 3. After hearing her story, I agreed with the psychiatrist's judgment. In fact, I went further, since I felt she not only *could not* but also *would not* remember the details of her sexual molestation.

Her memories were interesting. In two specific instances, she could remember up to a certain point but then could go no further. The story involved an elderly man, Uncle Arthur, whom she loved dearly. Rejected, and almost abandoned by her own parents, she felt he was the only person who really loved and cared for her. They were close friends and she remembered all sorts of wonderful things they did together. But there were two dark clouds in the blue skies of her memories. In one she remembered her upstairs bedroom. She could describe it in intricate detail—the wallpaper, the location of the furniture, her dolls. And she remembered one night when Uncle Arthur came into her bedroom and . . . Whenever she talked about this she became terribly agitated and emotional, but could remember nothing more. The other vivid picture was of something they often did together—pick blackberries. She talked in detail about the place, the woods, about filling the pails and carrying them home. But then her face grew dark and she would experience that same trembling turbulence as she tried to go on. She remembered trying to run with the pails full of berries . . . and then blank again.

After careful listening and questioning, I did something I rarely do. I told her what I felt sure was the obvious ending to each incident. I asked her to go home and spend some hours literally forcing her mind to remember what she was refusing to recall. Then she should come back the next day when I would hear the "rest of the story." She protested but finally agreed. She said she realized both her sanity and her marriage were on the brink of breakdown, unless she could come to terms with this inner turmoil.

She returned the next morning greatly perturbed. She had indeed had to force her mind to bring together the endings and the beginnings of both incidents and it was almost more than she could bear. Slowly, so slowly, she described all the details of Uncle Arthur's sex play with her. During prayer she literally relived those traumatic incidents. It was terribly painful. But there was a deeper level of agony which was the real issue. As the Lord took us back to her childhood, she sobbed it out in the voice of a little girl, *"O Uncle Arthur, why did you do that to me? You were all I had. I loved you more than anything else in the whole world. I loved you and I trusted you. How could you do that to me when I trusted you?"*

The real hurt was the betrayal of love and trust. After all the disappointments and rejections she had experienced from the important adults in her life, she had finally learned to love and trust someone. *And he too had betrayed her.* This was why her mind simply refused to put the stories together. *She did not want to have to believe this about one who she loved so much.* Certainly the sexual violation was a trauma. But her real battle was to forgive this betrayal and to allow God to restore trust in her and, also, to stop getting even with Uncle Arthur (and all men) through her relationship with her husband. We spent an unusually long time together in prayer and God answered in a remarkably deep and beautiful way. This was obvious when I received this letter:

I want to thank you for your part in my healing. It was the grand finale for me of many months of such struggle. You were God's instrument to help me possess the freedom He had promised me. And I am so enjoying my freedom. I know I have so much to learn and so does Tony, but oh, it is so great to be able to breathe fresh air after the stale foul air of the prison I was in. Freedom brings such delight to my soul. It has sort of put Tony in a state of shock—but I think he'll survive!

I guess I don't quite appreciate what my freedom means to him. After such a unique time Saturday night in our physical bonding, he gave his personal testimony in his Sunday School class the next morning. (Author's comment—I'd love to have heard that testimony!) I was not there but have been told by others he shared a lot about what's happened to me (not

my past, etc.) and then ended up crying in front
of everyone. Do you know, I have never seen
him cry. He has not told me about it yet, but
I'm sure he will. I wonder what God is doing in
his life through all of this. I praise Him for His
work in my life and in Tony's life. And His
work through your life.

A hug and a prayer for you.

In His Love,

Vangy

We have shared together several incidents which I trust
have driven home the central thrust of this chapter—to
always watch for the deeper issue of which the sexual
trauma is one important part. We do this by being prayerfully sensitive to the human spirit of the person sharing
and to the Holy Spirit who is guiding us to all truth.

In chapter 5 I referred to Dr. James Pennebaker's research on the relationship between confession and physical health. An update on these experiments has just been
published and is very relevant to our subject. In *The Lexington Herald-Leader*, Lexington, Kentucky, January 19,
1985, an article states, "Pennebaker has found that the
effect of inhibiting feelings was especially striking in people who underwent traumatic sexual experiences before
they were seventeen, people likely to be punished if they
talked about their feelings. As a result, Pennebaker said,
'They're more prone to reporting every kind of disease
imaginable—colds, flu, backaches, kidney problems,
cancer.' "

How important it is that we develop the wisdom, skill,
and spiritual resources to help the victims of sexual traumas find wholeness of body, mind, and spirit!

12

FOLLOW-UP, CAUTIONS, AND CONCLUSIONS

ONE OF THE CHIEF OBSTACLES to healing is our obsession with the immediate. The "itch for the instantaneous" pervades much of our Christian thinking. We tend to think that unless a healing is immediate, it is not of God and therefore not a "miracle." We have become impatient and frustrated with things that take time. The truth is that God Himself is going to slow down our pace, for He has no shortcuts to spiritual growth and maturity. Following the crisis of memory healing, the very important *process* of relearning and reprogramming needs to take place.

The most destructive result of repressed and unhealed memories is the way in which they have distorted our perceptions and pushed us into the wrong techniques of coping with life. Now that the painful sting has been removed from such memories, we still face the difficult task of forming new ways of relating to God, others, and ourselves. But now we are in a much better position to accomplish this. Why? Because we have a clearer comprehension of some of the forces which were previously pushing us into feelings and behavior we couldn't understand. It is true that simply having new insights will not necessarily give us a new life. But having those insights does enable us to identify more precisely the places in our personalities where we need to do the most praying and exercise the most discipline.

We need to see the whole picture. Prayer and discipline by themselves don't work for many until they have first undergone the healing of memories. In the same way, the healing prayer time by itself won't work without the follow-up afterward. For these people, true wholeness requires both. It would be impossible for me to exaggerate the importance of the follow-up time for counselors and counselees.

It will be profitable to turn back to chapter 9 and review the list of recommended books. Many of those can be very helpful in changing and rebuilding lives. In addition to that list, I can strongly recommend many of the books by the following authors:

A.W. Tozer	Bruce Narramore	Paul Tournier
James Dobson	Catherine Marshall	Charles Colson
C.S. Lewis	Dietrich Bonhoeffer	Norman Wright
Earl Jabay	E. Stanley Jones	Gary Collins
Larry Crabb	Charles Swindoll	

These authors have an excellent blending of biblical truth, psychological insight, and common sense. Most of us need all we can get of these three elements if we are to change our neurotic patterns of living! Pastors and counselors should also assist people in working out regular plans for Bible reading and memorization.

Another very valuable resource for renewing thought patterns is found in the great hymns and Gospel songs of our evangelical heritage. Making the effort to memorize them so they can be recalled in the hour of temptation and struggle will prove to be very worthwhile.

Some evangelicals are prejudiced against written prayers. Yet I have found books of prayers to be invaluable in teaching people constructive ways of praying. Among the most helpful are the prayers by Peter and Catherine Marshall. Perhaps the finest of all is John Baillie's A Diary of Private Prayer.

Many people need to follow their memory healing by developing new relationships through participation in a small-group fellowship. Here is where the church can function best as the healing body of Christ. Certain wounds are so deep that there will never be complete healing and reprogramming except in a support group which loves and accepts us as we are, and also cares enough to confront us into becoming what we need to be. Sometimes this is the greatest need during follow-up time—admitting we cannot do it alone and receiving the encouragement to risk opening ourselves up to a group of "healed helpers."

Changing Our Thought Patterns

Changing the way we think is essential. What follows is an article I give to many people who have difficulty overcoming low self-esteem and absurd, perfectionistic thought patterns. It contrasts right and wrong ways of perceiving relationships and will assist in "the process of transformation through the renewal of our minds."

THE PROCESS OF TRANSFORMATION THROUGH THE RENEWAL OF OUR MINDS

A partial list of the false, absurd, and unrealistic assumptions which contribute greatly to perfectionistic hangups and which need changing if healing is to take place.

A partial list of true, realistic, and biblical assumptions to replace the absurd ones. "Putting off the old and putting on the new" (Colossians 3:9-10) is part of the reprogramming so vital to the healing of our perfectionism.

MYSELF

1. I should be liked/approved of/loved by everybody, especially those I consider important to me.
2. I ought to be able to do anything/everything well—if I can't, it is better not to do it at all or to wait until I can.
3. I must be perfectly competent and successful in achieving before I consider myself worthwhile and before others do.
4. I really don't have control over my happiness—it is under the control of others and outside circumstances.
5. The experiences/influences of the past cannot be changed.
6. There is only **one** true/perfect solution for every problem—if I don't find it, I am sunk/lost/will be destroyed.
7. I ought to be able to make/keep everybody around me happy—if I don't, there is something wrong with me.
8. It is my responsibility to right

MYSELF and OTHERS

1. I am a worthwhile person whether I am successful in certain achievements or not.
   A. God has given His opinion of my value and worthwhileness.
   Psalm 8; Romans 5:6-8
   B. God's view on "success" is different from people's view.
   Luke 10:17-24; 1 Corinthians 1:25-31
   C. God has eliminated both comparison and competition and asks only "faithfulness" in exercising my particular gift(s).
   Luke 14:7-11; Matthew 20:1-16; 25:14-30; 1 Corinthians 12:4-27; Romans 12:6; Acts 5:29
2. I do not have to be approved/liked/loved by everyone in order to feel secure or lovable.
   A. Some people can't like/love me because of **their** problems.

the wrongs of the world/solve its problems/correct all injustices.

OTHERS

1. Others should take care of me/be kind to me/never frustrate me.

2. Others ought to be able to read my mind and know what I need/want without me telling them—if they can't do this, it is because they don't really like/love me.

GOD

1. God only accepts/loves me when He can approve everything I am/think/feel/say/do.

2. God may accept me as I am, but only because in the future I will never think/feel/say/do anything wrong.

3. God saves me by grace, but only maintains this relationship if I read/pray/witness/serve/do enough.

4. God holds my ultimate salvation in suspense—at the Great White Throne, He will judge me and then determine whether or not I will be given eternal life/heaven.

John 15:18-27; 17:14-19; Galatians 1:10; 4:12-16; 1 Peter 4:12-16; 1 John 3:11-13

B. Since I am always loved by God (regardless of how some may feel about me), I do not need to be overly concerned about the approval/disapproval of others.
John 15:9-10; 17:25-26; Romans 8; Hebrews 13:5-6; 1 John 4:16-19

GOD

1. God accepts/loves me even though He does not always approve of everything I do.
John 3:16-17; Romans 5:6-8; 1 John 4:7-10

2. Faith in what He has done for me (in Christ), not perfect performance, is what pleases God and puts/keeps me in a right(eous) relationship with Him.
Romans 1-5; Galatians; Hebrews 11:6

3. God, through His Holy Spirit, gives me the assurance of my salvation/eternal life/heaven now—my judgment took place on the cross. My only future judgment will be for service rewards and not for my salvation.
John 3:36; 5:24; 1 Corinthians 3:10-15; 1 John 3:24; 5:6-13

Rewriting Our Autobiographies

Perhaps the most difficult task after our memories have been healed is *integrating them into our total life.* Memory healing does *not* mean we no longer remember our past. To begin with, this would deny the very aim we have worked so hard to achieve—remembering everything, including the most painful experiences we've tried hard to forget. Also, it would be unscriptural. The Bible doesn't tell us to forget our past in that sense. Memory healing means being delivered from the prison of past hurts. We remember, but in a different way. *We cannot change the facts we remember, but we can change their meanings and the power they have over our present way of living.* This is where follow-up counseling can be most valuable—to help people discover meaning and purpose in their lives. Too often we have taken Romans 8:28 out of its total context. We need to remember just where that great verse appears—it follows the two verses about inner healing we have quoted so often, Romans 8:26-27.

> The Spirit also helps our weakness; for we do not know how to pray as we should, but the Spirit Himself intercedes for us with groanings too deep for words; and He who searches the hearts knows what the mind of the Spirit is, because He intercedes for the saints according to the will of God.
>
> And we know that God causes all things to work together for good to those who love God, to those who are called according to His purpose.

A major part of the healing process is the discovery that God can take even the most painful of our experiences and work them out for our good and His glory. As we have said before, this does not mean God is the *Author* of everything that has happened to us. But it does mean He is the *Master* of it all. And during the follow-up sessions we help people rewrite their autobiographies by seeing and assigning new meanings to even the most painful incidents—the meanings God is going to work out through them. People who have been healed have often told me how *God is now using them to bring healing to others who have suffered similar experiences.* In effect, they have learned to say what Joseph said to his brothers, "You meant evil against me, but God meant it for good" (Genesis 50:20).

Learning How To Heal Memories on Our Own

A final word regarding the follow-up sessions. We should work with people to help them learn the basic principles of memory healing. Then they can use this form of prayer therapy with their spouse or a trusted friend. Counselors are temporary assistants to the Holy Spirit. They should aim at putting themselves out of a job as quickly as possible. Husbands or wives, friends, or small share-groups should someday take their place, and ultimately, Christians should learn to take hurtful memories directly to the Great Counselor, the Holy Spirit, and receive His healing.

Memory Healing as Preventive Medicine

Thus far we have talked about this form of inner healing as a kind of spiritual surgery. As parents, we can also learn to use it as *prayer therapy in reverse. That is, when we sense our children have been hurt by the accidents and traumas of life, we can help them open up their feelings to us and pray for their healing as a form of preventive therapy.* In this way their hurts and humiliations will not turn to hates and hits and we can keep them emotionally and spiritually healthy. Hundreds of parents have shared with me that a new sensitivity toward their children's hurts is one of the best serendipities of their own healing of memories.

Cautions and Conclusions

From the very beginning we have stressed that memory healing is *one and only one form of spiritual therapy.* I have written this book with much hesitation. My greatest fear is that some will try to use it as a gimmick, a quick and easy answer to emotional/spiritual problems. Or that they will consider it the answer for everyone. Let me say it with unbecoming intensity—THE HEALING OF MEMORIES IS NOT A CURE-ALL FOR EVERY EMOTIONAL AND SPIRITUAL HANGUP. In fact, under no circumstances should it be used with certain types of problems and personality types. It is most useful and successful with people who have severely repressed the memories of their most painful experiences and have thus tended to become closed and unable to express their true feelings about God, others, and themselves. As a result, they have then become withdrawn and unable to form close and intimate interpersonal relationships. With such persons, sometimes known as "God's Frozen Chosen," it can bring release from buried resentments, forgiveness, and the freedom to move on to genuine emotional and spiritual maturity.

However, *it should not be used with certain kinds of extremely emotional and hysteric types of people.* I have often begun counseling with people whom I felt might need healing for bad memories. However, when I asked for

their written list, they have brought back great, lengthy
epistles with hundreds of minor incidents described in the
minutest details. These people proved not to have memories and emotions which were repressed or locked in.
They had quite the opposite problem. Everything was
blown way out of proportion and surrounded with all
kinds of fantasy emotions. So, I have had to reverse my
original plan and help such people learn *how to control
undisciplined and unruly emotions which were creating havoc
in their lives.* To attempt something like the healing of
memories with such persons only further stirs up the un-
controlled emotions and can result in increased disequilib-
rium. It can literally do more harm than good. These
individuals need a much more rational kind of counseling.
They don't need help in contacting *unexpressed emotions*;
rather they must be taught how to control *unruly emotions.* I share this in the hope that no one will make
memory healing a kind of spiritual fad, or quickie emotional cure-all.

As we conclude, we discover we have come full circle.
We began with mystery and we end with it. There are
some things we know about healing of memories; there
are some things we do not know. Certainly there have
been enough positive and miraculous results in people's
lives to encourage us in seeking further truth about it.
There are also enough negatives to make us issue cautions. No one will ever fully fathom the mystery of memory, anymore than we will ever fully understand the mystery of God in whose image we have been created. So let
us walk humbly before the Lord, asking His Holy Spirit to
keep guiding us into the truth which sets us free. In the
meantime, let us use the wisdom He has given us, in the
spirit of Moses, who said, "The secret things belong to
the Lord our God, but the things revealed belong to us

and to our sons forever, that we may observe all the words
of this Law" (Deuteronomy 29:29).

Dear Reader:

We would like to know your opinion of **Healing of Memories.** Your ideas will help us as we strive to continue offering books that will satisfy your needs and interests.

Send your responses to:
    VICTOR BOOKS
    1825 College Avenue
    Wheaton, IL 60187

What most influenced your decision to purchase this book?
- ☐ Front Cover
- ☐ Title
- ☐ Author
- ☐ Back cover material
- ☐ Price
- ☐ Length
- ☐ Subject
- ☐ Other: _____

What did you like about this book?
- ☐ Helped me understand myself better
- ☐ Helped me understand others better
- ☐ Helped me understand the Bible
- ☐ Helped me understand God
- ☐ It was easy to teach
- ☐ Author
- ☐ Good reference tool

How was this book used?
- ☐ For my personal reading
- ☐ Studied it in a group situation
- ☐ Used it to teach a group
- ☐ As a reference tool
- ☐ For a church or school library

If you used this book to teach a group, did you also use the accompanying leader's guide? ☐ YES ☐ NO

Please indicate your level of interest in reading other Victor Books like this one.
- ☐ Very interested
- ☐ Somewhat interested
- ☐ Not very interested
- ☐ Not at all interested

Would you recommend this book to a friend? ☐ YES ☐ NO

Please indicate your age.
- ☐ Under 18
- ☐ 18-24
- ☐ 25-34
- ☐ 35-44
- ☐ 45-54
- ☐ 55 or over

Would you like to receive more information about Victor Books? If so, please fill in your name and address.

NAME: _____

ADDRESS: _____

_____

Do you have additional comments or suggestions regarding Victor Books?